3000 LESBIANS GO TO YORK

Also by Jane Traies

The Lives of Older Lesbians: Sexuality, Identity and the Life Course

Now You See Me: Lesbian Life Stories

Free to Be Me: Refugee Stories from the Lesbian Immigration Support Group

3000 LESBIANS GO TO YORK

THE STORY OF A QUEER ARTS FESTIVAL

JANE TRAIES

Tollington

*In memory of Claire Mooney
(1956–2024)
who set the festival to music*

~

First published in 2025 by Tollington Press, Machynlleth, Wales
www.tollingtonpress.co.uk

Copyright © Jane Traies 2025
Jane Traies asserts the moral right
to be identified as the author of this work.

All rights reserved. No part of this book may be reproduced or
transmitted, in any form or by any means, without permission.

A catalogue record for this book is available from the British Library.

ISBN 978-1-909347-30-4

Designed and typeset by Helen Sandler
Printed and bound in the UK by Mixam

CONTENTS

Introduction	7
Opening a Women's Bookshop	13
Not a Disco Type	28
A Lesbian Book Festival	33
It All Started in York	50
Lesbian Pride at the Racecourse	53
An Impertinent Question	66
Publish and Perish	68
A Celebration Like Never Before	71
Silver Rings	92
Rescuing the Festival	99
A Sapphic Idyll	115
Writers & Readers	127
A Weekend on Planet Dyke	145
Family Feelings	154
Making It Work for Everyone	157
Fighting to Survive	171
Legacies	191
In the Company of Lesbians	204
List of Authors and Performers	208
Acknowledgements and Image Credits	210
'Now a Major Motion Picture'	212
About the Author	224

Libertas! bookstall at the festival *(Lenna Cumberbatch)*

INTRODUCTION

'DIDN'T WE MEET IN YORK?'

It's a question I'm still asked – and the answer is always yes – because, for a legendary decade between 1998 and 2008, the city of York was the epicentre of lesbian arts and culture in the UK. Each autumn, thousands of women flocked to the Lesbian Arts Festival there, to meet their favourite authors, buy books, hear top female singers and bands, socialise and dance the night away at the 'disco of a thousand lesbians'. Looking through old festival programmes is like taking a tour of lesbian culture in the Noughties.

Nowadays, though, I often talk to younger women who have never heard of the York Lesbian Arts Festival, or of Libertas!, the bookshop that gave birth to it. So this book is an attempt to capture that piece of our history while it still lives in memory; to bring those glorious times back to life for those of us who were there; and to give a flavour of the festival to those who missed it or are too young to remember it. Dozens of women – writers and performers, volunteers and faithful fans – have contributed to the book, either in recorded interviews or in writing. Others have sent me photos, programmes, tickets and precious memorabilia. Together, we have pieced together the story of a festival that is still remembered with affection by thousands of lesbian, bi and queer women today.

Inevitably, this book holds my own memories, too. In 2001, my then partner Jacky Bratton and I had just published our second historical novel under the joint pseudonym Jay Taverner. Out of the blue, we received an email from Jenny Roberts at Libertas! inviting us to read at 'the UK's biggest lesbian book festival ever'. It was pretty much our first piece of public recognition, so we were thrilled, and accepted at once.

It felt extraordinary, slightly unreal, to be surrounded by those fabulous authors in whose books we were seeing ourselves represented at last. The first person we met when we arrived outside St John's College on that grey November day was Sarah Waters. I remember telling her, rather shyly, how much I had enjoyed her latest novel, *Affinity*. I don't remember our own contribution at all, though the programme tells me that Jay Taverner spoke on a historical writing panel with Sarah, alongside Rose Collis.

What I do remember vividly is the crime-writing panel. Jenny had asked me to be a moderator. ('You were a teacher, weren't you, Jane? So you know how to keep people in order.') I found myself onstage in that enormous hall, with an audience of 400 women and a panel made up of some of the best-known and -loved writers there: Val McDermid, whose lesbian detective Lindsay Gordon had already solved half a dozen cases; Manda Scott, creator of the Kellen Stewart series; Stella Duffy, who had brought out her fourth Saz Martin novel the year before; and our host, Jenny Roberts herself, who introduced us to her own lesbian detective, Cameron McGill. A daunting quartet, to say the least – and I don't think I 'kept them in order' in any way!

Opposite: Jane Traies (left) and Jacky Bratton, 2002 *(Kim Watson)*
Above: College of Ripon and York St John (now a university)

While I was in awe of every one of them, they already knew each other from their appearances at numerous book festivals, and they certainly knew how to entertain an audience without any help from me. Nonetheless, I was completely hooked. In one role or another, I was at every festival after that.

As the Libertas! Lesbian Book Festival went on to become the York Lesbian Arts Festival (YLAF) and an iconic piece of lesbian history, it also became an important part of my life. After Jacky and I parted in 2005, Jay Taverner was no longer a participating author, but by then I was part of the organising committee and, later, the board of trustees. So, at a time when the rest of my life was unstable, YLAF was a constant. Over the years, I did a variety of jobs: managing the marketplace, running the Friends' scheme, assisting Helen Sandler when she was Festival Director and so on. Being part of the festival brought me into contact with all sorts of people, many of whom are still good friends. Making this book has been a walk down Memory Lane.

But the story starts well before I was ever involved. It begins, not with a festival, but with a ground-breaking bookshop. ∎

1998-2000

Above: Val McDermid (left) and Jenny Roberts at the shop opening
Below: Surrounded by fans and copies of the aptly named *Star Struck*

OPENING A WOMEN'S BOOKSHOP

IF YOU WERE LIVING in York in November 1998, it would have been hard to ignore the arrival of Libertas! On opening day, the queue of would-be customers for this new women's bookshop stretched halfway down Gillygate. Inside, the colourful space was already packed to capacity. Glasses of bubbly were handed round, and novelist Val McDermid officially declared Libertas! open. Val still has a vivid memory of that day:

> Years and years ago, I met Jenny Roberts in York, and she said, 'I'm going to open a lesbian bookshop!'
> And I thought, this woman is mad.
> But she wasn't mad: she went ahead and founded Libertas! I was there to open the shop, and that was an astonishing experience. I turned up on the day with my partner and her sister (who's also a lesbian) and I thought there would be about six people there. It was packed! It was full of women, all sorts of shapes, sizes, colours – it was a kaleidoscope of lesbians, if you like – and it was a shop full of books about women. It was an amazing experience to be in a space like that. I'd been in women's bookshops in the States, but this was different. This was our territory, our turf. And there were all sorts of people there – some I'd known for years and didn't even know they were lesbians!
> So, it was a lovely experience. And the warmth in the room was extraordinary. People were just so excited. There was that sense of a place where we could be ourselves, but also where we had all these books available to us – instead of going into a bookshop and finding the LGBT section stuck in the back, and most of them books about men.

The official opening was followed by a day-long programme of events, as the first customers were steadily replaced from the apparently endless queue. Hundreds of people visited the shop that day: Ann Murray, a Canadian who was one of the first assistants, described the atmosphere as 'buzzing'. Ann also claims the distinction of thinking up the shop's name: liber is Latin for 'a book', and libertas means 'freedom'.

The celebrations continued into the evening with a lavish women-only event at York's Grand Assembly Rooms. Invitations had been sent to lesbian social groups and organisations all across Yorkshire and the North East; 300 women attended. They were entertained until late into the night by a line-up of female musicians, headed by singer-songwriter Claire Mooney.

'I live in Manchester,' Claire told me, 'so I don't know how Jenny knew me, except that I'd been playing forever! And I was always involved, somehow, after that. Every year.' The opening night raised £1300 for breast cancer research and £700 for Lesbian Line in Yorkshire, and was excitedly reported in the local press.

The driving force behind all this activity, Jenny Roberts,

L to R: Jenny, Jen, Yvonne, Claire and Sue having fun onstage at the opening party at the Assembly Rooms (*Jenny Roberts*)

had arrived in York only a couple of years before, and Libertas! was to be an important part of making a life for herself there. The shop would be Jenny's way of saying 'thank you' to the community that she felt had welcomed her so kindly when she moved to the city after her gender transition in 1996:

> Such a good life! I had lots of lesbian friends, who I'd got to know very quickly in the Over-35s Lesbian Social Group. And all the people on my street were so friendly, too. I felt I'd really been welcomed into the women's community. And I wanted to give something back.

Jenny had some capital from the sale of the printing business she'd run in her previous life, and decided to use it to open a women's bookshop.

It was, to put it mildly, a challenging time to attempt such a thing. Small independent booksellers were closing down all over the country: only one women's bookshop – Silver Moon in London – was still in business. The Conservative government that had created such a hostile environment for LGBTQ people with Section 28 of the Local Government Act

Libertas! shop window (JR)

ten years before was still in power. (Under Section 28, local authorities were forbidden to 'promote' homosexuality, or 'the teaching in any maintained school of the acceptability of homosexuality as a pretended family relationship'.) There was still a ban on lesbians, gay men and bi people serving in the armed forces. Most lesbians, especially teachers, nurses and others working in the public sector, were firmly in the closet.

Undeterred by any of these things – or perhaps determined to fight them – Jenny went about her plan with characteristic energy and thoroughness, visiting Silver Moon and other alternative bookshops, talking to publishers like The Women's Press and meeting with wholesalers. The advice she received, from publishers and booksellers alike, was 'Tread carefully!' Women's bookshops, they implied, had had their day.

But Jenny was on a mission. When she felt she understood enough about the trade, she looked for suitable premises, and found them at 42 Gillygate, one of a row of shops in central York not far from the Minster. A design team was brought in to advise on the décor, colour scheme, literature and window displays; women decorators painted the walls in the Suffragette colours of purple and green. The process was not without its challenges, however. Two days before she moved into the new premises, Jenny received a letter

Shop staff in the early days (opposite) and the core team in 2001 (above, L to R): Nick, Chrissy, Jenny and Ann *(JR)*

from the shopfitting company that had agreed to provide all the shelving, saying they were unable to deliver what she had asked for. When she phoned to ask what the problem was, one of the firm's partners told her: 'We don't deal with businesses like yours.'

It wasn't a complete surprise. As Jenny calmly explained to journalist Vicky Anning ('What Women Want,' *Guardian* 8/12/98): 'I'm quite prepared for problems. A lot of conventional people can't get their heads round anything alternative. People are a bit frightened of it.' Opposition was not going to stop her.

From the beginning, the Libertas! project was about visibility and about claiming space for women and lesbians. 'At the time, most lesbian events were in fairly grotty places like back rooms,' Jenny remembers. But she believed her customers deserved better: hence the glamorous choice of venue for the opening night party. In those days, the beautiful Grand Assembly Rooms in York were occupied by a high-end traditional restaurant, and Jenny remembers that the manager was openly worried about the nature of the clientèle that Libertas! might attract. To his surprise, however, his prejudices were quickly put to rest by the friendly good manners of the

Ann Croft (JR)

women who attended; he was especially charmed, Jenny told me, by the way they helpfully collected up the glasses at the end of the evening. 'So the opening night went really well. And it was so unusual, because it was a really beautiful ballroom, and everything was perfect!' Libertas! and its lesbian customers had arrived in York, in style.

The bookshop was immediately popular. Ann Murray describes it as 'light and bright – all very welcoming. It was a cornucopia: fiction, non-fiction, mystery, romance, biography, poetry, travel, women's studies – you name it! There was something here for everyone, all lovingly arranged.' Women of all ages spent hours there, browsing and chatting. Although it advertised itself as a women's bookshop, Libertas! rapidly became better known as a safe space for lesbians. Festival-goer Margaret Bird remembers it as 'a great haven in York at that time'. The shop assistants often found themselves acting as confidantes and informal counsellors. 'Some people said I was the first person that they had confided in,' Ann Murray remembers.

Hilary Nowell, who with her partner Pauline was to become a regular visitor, remembers the excitement of going into Libertas!:

> It was lovely. You felt alive. It was like going into a sweetshop. They were so personal and hands-on; you could chat about anything to them. I'd have hated to have gone in and not bought anything – but at the same time, you really needed a lock on your wallet, to stop you from buying up the shop!

Libertas! tried hard to maintain its identity as a shop for all women, stocking feminist and women's political titles. However, it quickly gained such a strong reputation as a lesbian space that straight women were sometimes reluctant to go in. Press coverage played a part in this, by foregrounding the lesbian and trans elements of the story. 'It soon became known as "that lesbian shop",' Jenny told me – adding, with a mischievous grin, 'We really liked that!'

On the Saturday after the opening, another Ann visited the shop for the first time. She came in with a friend – a brave move, as she was not yet out as a lesbian and must have felt quite shy. But Ann Croft was soon to play a huge role in Libertas! and its future development – as well as in Jenny's life. It was not until the following year that they met socially; by the end of that year, they were a couple. A few months later, Ann joined the staff at Libertas! She worked mainly in the office, but also took shifts behind the counter to give Jenny time to write.

Playing to their lesbian readers, who rapidly became their core customer base, Libertas! had started a mail order service, together with a newsletter, *Dykelife*, publicising new stock. In 2000, Ann took over the newsletter and was soon writing and distributing it every other month. It was hard work, she remembers:

See no evil... 'Evening of Crime' with (L to R) Alma Fritchley, Val McDermid, Manda Scott (JR)

When we were doing *Dykelife*, we sometimes went home at two o'clock in the morning. The printer was just across the road, and we'd put it through their letterbox as we left. We did produce it every month for a short while, but we soon gave that up and reverted to every two months!

As another way to increase the sale of books (which even then had a notoriously low profit margin), Libertas! started to arrange readings and events. The first of these, the 'Virago Roadshow', was held at the Grange Hotel, a beautiful Regency building in central York, in 1999. The second was an 'Evening of Lesbian Crime', featuring Val McDermid, Alma Fritchley and Manda Scott, all three of whom would go on to become stalwarts of the later festivals. Manda remembers how that evening came about. By this stage, not just books, but videos, cards and calendars were posted out from the shop to customers all over the country, and she phoned to order a calendar:

> I was giving them my credit card details, and they said, 'Oh, are you that Manda Scott? Do you write books?'
> I think I was on the second of the Kellen Stewart books then, so I said, 'Yes.'
> And they said, 'Would you like to come and do an event?'
> So I said, 'Nobody'll come if it's just me. You'll have to get Val McDermid.'
> And that's how it started.

The evening was fun, Val remembers:

> It was quite a posh place to do it. Lesbian readings then usually ended up in the basement of something else. So, right from the start, that was a marker, that Jenny Roberts was not going to settle for second best for lesbians. And that was one of the hallmarks of that time: a few women who very strongly believed that lesbians had a right to

the best spaces, the best of everything. Jenny definitely carried that idea through, in those readings and beyond.

That same year, a new feminist publishing imprint, Raw Nerve Books, was set up at the Centre for Women's Studies at the University of York. Its mission was to publish innovative and controversial books in the fields of gender and women's studies. One of the founders, Ann Kaloski, reflected at the time:

> York is a surprisingly good place for those interested in women's writing and feminist issues. We have the Centre at the University, the bookshop Libertas!, a growing women's dance scene, a packed programme around International Women's Day in March, and now Raw Nerve Books. *(University press release, November 1998)*

Their first title was launched at the shop; their second at King's Manor – the lovely medieval building used by the university – again with assistance from Libertas! 'Jenny was really supportive,' Ann Kaloski remembers.

Meanwhile, Jenny had submitted her crime novel *Needle Point* to another new imprint: Diva Books, a spinoff from *Diva* magazine. The commissioning editor, Helen Sandler, was on the lookout for new lesbian writers of all ages, and snapped up Jenny's manuscript. Later that year, encouraged by the success of the Libertas! events so far, Jenny, Helen, and their colleagues collaborated on the 'Diva Books Roadshow',

to be held on a Saturday afternoon at the College of Ripon and York St John. Tickets sold fast, and on 25 November 2000 an audience of a hundred women gathered to hear a diverse group of writers reading from recent Diva Books publications.

The opening session featured authors Lee Maxwell (*Emerald Budgies*); VG Lee (*The Comedienne*) and Jenny Roberts herself (*Needle Point*). Then Kathleen Kiirik Bryson introduced the audience to the three heroines of *Mush*, her novel set in Alaska. After a break, there was a discussion based on some of the issues raised in *girl2girl*, a groundbreaking book written by and for very young lesbian and bi women, edited by Norrina Rashid and Jane Hoy. The last panel was a trio of authors whose work had appeared in *The Diva Book of Short Stories*: local Yorkshire writers Sue Vickerman and Linda Innes, and Helen herself, who had edited the collection.

At a time when fiction about lesbians was still dominated by American titles, Helen recalls it felt important to be publishing a UK anthology. 'We wanted to celebrate a really contemporary style of writing,' she says, 'and some of the stories came from brand-new writers via a public callout. The book went on to win a Lambda Literary Award in the States, so that showed we could give the Americans a run for their money!'

Libertas! also sold DVDs and the afternoon concluded with a screening of one of these: the new coming-out movie, *Pourquoi pas moi? (Why Not Me?)*. In the evening, a disco featuring Mad Mandy (a DJ Jenny had met through a lesbian social group in Leeds) was enjoyed by audience and authors alike.

Encouraged by the resounding success of the Diva Books Roadshow – and by the number of books sold at it – Jenny quickly decided that the following year she would expand the concept, with more authors and a bigger audience. And so the idea of a lesbian book festival was born. ∎

Above: VG Lee (right) and friend Gina outside the shop

Right: Jenny Roberts with display of her debut novel *Needle Point*

The hunger for lesbian books was clear from packed events not only at Libertas! but at launches round the country for the *Diva Book of Short Stories*

Waterstones Piccadilly, London, clockwise from right: Editor Helen Sandler with contributor Kathleen Bryson (soon to join her on the staff of Diva Books); standing room only; authors Stella Duffy, Emma Donoghue and Ali Smith

Below: Waterstones Manchester (L to R): Rosie Lugosi, Jackie Kay, Helen Sandler, Helen Smith, Cathy Bolton and Jo Somerset

Not a Disco Type
Jane Anderson-Hawkes

I saw the book festival advertised when I went into Libertas! one day and thought it would be fun. (What's not to like? It was all about books and lesbians!) I'd just come out of a difficult relationship and was feeling a bit bruised. I really needed some fun and thought it might give me a way to meet new friends.

My friend and I got to York a bit early, so we went into the gay pub on Gillygate to wait for everything to start at St John's. We were talking about looking forward to the afternoon, when this woman walked in, and the only place spare to sit down was next to us. And that's the first time I met my future wife, Anna.

After about half an hour we left. Anna was meeting up with friends, so we said goodbye and hoped we might see each other at St John's. We had a great afternoon, listening to the authors. During the coffee breaks I saw Anna another couple of times and we enjoyed chatting with each other. I thought she seemed really nice, but that was it. I wasn't looking for another relationship at that point.

I loved the readings and thoroughly enjoyed spending time at a venue that was full of like-minded people. St John's felt cosy and personal. I've also got a soft spot for it because it's where I met Anna.

Once the readings were over, I wasn't that worried about going to the disco afterwards. I'm not a disco type of person and I also had three children who were being looked after by my ex-husband. But I'd come with a friend and didn't want to spoil her fun, so I stayed. I'm glad I did!

FESTIVAL STORY

I'm not hugely sociable, so I mostly just watched and I couldn't take my eyes off Anna. She's a real dancer and she absolutely loves it. She can really move. In between dancing until she dropped, she kept coming and sitting next to me and we attempted to talk despite the noisy music. I found myself looking forward to her coming over to sit next to me again throughout the evening.

When it was time to leave, we walked to the car park together and I remember thinking that, whilst I didn't want a relationship, she was someone I would like to keep in touch with, so I took courage and asked her for her phone number. She, too, was just out of a challenging relationship, so both of us were very cautious. Nevertheless, she agreed to give me her phone number. We started seeing each other a week or so after that first meeting. And we went to YLAF every year after that.

We have now been together for 24 years. We've had a fair few tragedies, but we've stuck together through it all and we have a good life together. ■

Above: Jane (left) and Anna outside St John's
Overleaf: Horse at 2002 concert *(Caroline Clark)*

2001-03

A LESBIAN BOOK FESTIVAL

THE FRONT PAGE OF *DYKELIFE* for May/June 2001 was full of news about the forthcoming Lesbian Book Festival – 'the UK's biggest ever' – to be held that November. Once again, the event was co-sponsored by *Diva* and was to be held at the College of Ripon and York St John; but this time it would last all day and would feature many more writers. Some twenty authors were already signed up: Jenny's aim was to invite every UK-based lesbian writer with a book in print. There would be an all-day bar, with food available, and in the evening, Mad Mandy would DJ at the 'Libertas! Third Birthday Party Women-only Disco'. Tickets were £7 for the festival and £5 for the disco. Jenny and Ann knew that many of their audience would come from a considerable distance, so included a list of local accommodation with any tickets posted to addresses outside York. (This was to become a tradition in the following years, and helped to draw many of York's accommodation providers into a positive relationship with their lesbian clientèle.)

It quickly became clear that there was an eager audience for this kind of event. The original 250 tickets sold out in a week. Jenny booked a second lecture room in the college, added more author panels to the programme and issued another 150 tickets. Two weeks later, they (and all the disco tickets) were sold, too. By now it was too late to find a bigger venue, but customers who'd been unable to get tickets were offered the chance to pre-order signed copies of books by any of the authors present. The excitement continued to build through the summer: *Dykelife* for July/August trumpeted, 'Val McDermid and Sandi Toksvig confirm for Book Festival!'

Running an event with two dozen speakers and 400 attendees required many helpers, but there was no shortage of volunteers. Not all came from York, either, but from the now-widespread community of Libertas! customers. Nic Herriot was living in mid-Wales, but was one of the first to step forward:

> I knew about Libertas! bookshop, and I was starting to get my books from there. When I found out about the festival, through *Diva*, I phoned up the bookshop and said, could I volunteer? And I would do any of the odd jobs that needed doing. Because I know at these kind of festivals they do need help. And also, that's the cheapest way to do it, when you're poor and a single parent!
>
> I arrived there, and I was given this ticket saying 'Runner'. Basically, I was a gopher. I did anything and everything. For example, in the main foyer there were tables with books for the authors to sign, but as they sold out, there was no one to get any new books. So I said, 'Tell me where they are? That's my job.' Then I would run to the stores, get more books, and put them on the authors' tables. There was a green room, and there were tea breaks, but the authors were always busy; so, 'Do you want a cup of tea?' and off I went and got cups of tea. And that was kind of what I did all day. Made myself useful. If anything was missing, I went and got it.
>
> So I was there right at the beginning. And I went on being involved, as a volunteer, from then on.

Another volunteer who was to become a permanent fixture was Elspeth Mallowan. She and her partner Liz lived in Sheffield, but some time before this had read about York's Over-35s Lesbian Social Group in *Diva* and decided to try it. They found a warm welcome there and started to attend regularly, which was how they met Jenny and Ann. Once Libertas! opened, they made a point of going to the bookshop whenever they were in York.

Elspeth Mallowan (front left) on timekeeping duty *(Lenna Cumberbatch)*

So, when Jenny asked for stewards and timekeepers for the festival, Elspeth was one of a group of eight or nine women to volunteer. 'And it was absolutely wonderful,' she remembers. 'So I was involved, right from the get-go.' Timekeeping became Elspeth's speciality from then on. As she explains:

> In each of the sessions there was a person responsible for housekeeping the practicalities of it. So I sat in and listened to authors that I wouldn't necessarily have done, and that broadened my horizons. The timekeepers held up cards to let the speakers know when they had ten minutes left, and then five minutes. They had strict instructions that, if the speaker didn't stop when warned, they were simply to stand up and start giving a vote of thanks!

In this way, Elspeth and her colleagues provided one of the organisational details that made this and all the later festivals work so well: panel sessions, almost without exception, started and ended on time.

Anne Rippon was another volunteer who was to prove an invaluable member of the core team through the years. She looked after security at the festivals, in a very professional

Above: Security and stewarding coordinator Anne Rippon *(LC)*
Below: Elizabeth Woodcraft and Charlotte Mendelson *(KW)*

manner, as Jenny remembers: 'Without Anne, it would have been very difficult to keep going. She was brilliant at keeping everything running smoothly – and tactfully turning away people who might cause a nuisance.'

And it meant a lot to Anne to be involved. She told me: 'I think about the festival every year, as October comes around, and remember all the great times.'

The single-sheet programme for the 2001 book festival includes almost every lesbian author in the UK who had a book in print at that time, from the established writers already mentioned to a group of 'new kids on the block' – Charlotte Mendelson, Shamim Sarif, Helen Shacklady and Elizabeth Woodcraft – who had recently published their first book. This egalitarian mixing of less well-known writers and (increasingly) well-known ones was to remain a feature of the festivals through the years. Charlotte Mendelson loved being there:

> There was something idyllic about Libertas! Particularly the first one I went to. It seemed astounding that there could be a festival, not only for fans and authors of women's literature, but for *lesbian* fiction... mind-blowing. I dimly remember it was in a more old-fashioned building than the ritzy but corporate Racecourse, and it felt like being at a women's college: united with fellow bluestockings, with a sexy frisson; the dream.

But, she adds:

> It's also a lost idyll; not only because it changed, but also because, for various reasons, I couldn't make the most of it. I couldn't meet enough new people or go to really niche events. There were so many fellow fiction enthusiasts and interesting women there, and I barely talked to any of them. I wish I could go back to the excitement and optimism of

Libertas! Lesbian Book Progr

10am to 10.30am Reception

Time	Temple Hall
10.35 am to 11.15 am *(Lecture Theatre 10.15 to 11.15)*	**WELCOME** - followed immediately by **IS THIS ANY SORT OF LIFE?** Val McDermid and Manda Scott ...discuss writing as a career
11.30 am to 12.30 pm	**YOU JUST GOTTA LAUGH.....** Helen Sandler, Alma Fritchley, V G Lee, Linda Innes ...talk about writing humour Moderated by: Rose Collis
1.15 pm to 2.15 pm	**GOING BACK IN TIME** Sarah Waters, Jay Taverner, Rose Collis ...talk about writing history Moderated by: VG Lee
3.00 pm to 4.00 pm	**PUTTING THE KNIFE IN** Val McDermid, Stella Duffy, Manda Scott, Jenny Roberts ...talk about writing crime Moderated by: Jay Taverner
4.30 pm to 5.30 pm	**SANDI TOKSVIG - SOLO** Television personality, writer, archaelogist, TV panelist and comedienne Sandi Toksvig talks about herself her writing and life.

Festival 2001

amme

& Coffee in the Crush Bar

Lecture Theatre

FAMILY AFFAIRS

Lisa Saffron talks about her new book 'It's a Family Affair' and leads a discussion about lesbian parenting
From 10.15 am to 11.15 am in the Lecture Theatre

NEW KIDS ON THE BLOCK

 Charlotte Mendelson   *Shamim Sarif*   *Helen Shacklady*   *Elizabeth Woodcraft*

...introduce their debut novels   Moderated by: Jay Taverner

WE CAN WORK IT OUT

 Caeia March   *Eleanor Hill*   *Jenny McKean Tinker*   *Jane Fletcher*

...talk about writing relationships   Moderated by: Ann Kaloski*

BREAKING THE RULES

 Ali Smith   *Kathleen Kiirik Bryson*   *Lee Maxwell*

...talk about unconventional writing   Moderated by: Helen Sandler

The Festival Bookstall will be open from 10 am until 6.30 pm in the foyer of the Main Hall. Authors will be available there to sign books immediately after their panel.

** **Ann Kaloski** teaches at the Centre for Women's Studies, University of York, has published various books on sexuality; cyber space; and popular culture and is co-director of the radical press, Raw Nerve Books.*

that first time, but as myself now: the more confident and open woman I've become.

There was indeed a lot to choose from: four sessions during the day, with two panels on offer each time, and breaks for book-buying and refreshments. In the opening sessions, Val McDermid and Manda Scott chatted about the writing life, while Lisa Saffron read from *It's a Family Affair* and led a discussion on lesbian parenting. This was an important political issue at a time when same-sex couples were not recognised as the legal parents of children conceived through donor insemination, and were not eligible to apply for joint adoption, either. Other sessions covered a variety of themes including humour, relationships, and experimental fiction, as well as history and crime-writing.

VG Lee, who had been part of the Diva Books Roadshow and was to appear at every one of the festivals that followed, read from her first novel, *The Comedienne*. She still remembers how worried she had been beforehand:

> We didn't know whether that first one was going to be a success or not. Everybody travelled from all over the country to get up to York. And then it was a rainy morning. We didn't know if anybody was going to turn up. But slowly, women started to drift in, and then at a certain point – I think it was about eleven in the morning – you suddenly realised that the room was full. And off we went! We were so excited. We were like children, really. We were just so happy, because we had a success and people liked us. They liked what we were doing.

After an afternoon tea break, the day was to culminate in an appearance by star guest Sandi Toksvig. During the break, when most of the volunteers were setting up the big hall for Sandi's session, 'gopher' Nic had been sitting in the entrance hall:

> I was just sitting there, chilling, and in comes Sandi Toksvig! So I got up and casually sauntered over, and I said, 'Hello, can I help you?'
>
> She said, 'I've come for the evening event.'
>
> And I said – God, I was dreadful! – 'Have you got a ticket?'
>
> And she went, 'Oh. Oh, erm...'
>
> So, of course I said, 'Sandi, it's all right! I know who you are! You're allowed in!'

Sandi was already well known as a TV presenter, comedian and writer (having just published *Flying Under Bridges*) and Jenny hadn't been entirely sure whether she could attract – or afford – such a star. But she recalls:

> I wrote to her publisher to ask if she could come, and Sandi wrote back herself and said she would love to. We could only offer her £50 towards her expenses, but she booked her own hotel. She's a wonderful woman and she wanted

Sandi Toksvig delighting the audience again the following year
(Caroline Clark)

to support people, particularly lesbians. She thought it was really important.

Sandi brought the house down with her opening line: 'Isn't it delightful to see how many women are serious about literature and not just here for a shag?' and then kept the audience laughing for an hour with tales of her life and writing. Festival-goer Jane Anderson-Hawkes has a particularly sharp memory of Sandi's set that night:

> Anna and I needed the loo but there was a big queue, so we went in one together. When we came out, Sandi was outside waiting to come in. You can imagine the comments she made – which she then repeated onstage. Made us laugh!

Finally, everyone danced the night away to the music of Mad Mandy and her mobile disco. Sarah Waters remembers: 'The venue was small; we were practically dancing round our handbags. It was a really good night.' For Elspeth Mallowan, it was 'absolutely fabulous'. Quite apart from the books, the

York by night *(Kate O'Dwyer)*

music and the dancing, an event such as this offered a very special sense of belonging, at a time when few queer people lived entirely open lives.

Many women's memories are imbued with an almost magical atmosphere. Christine Webb, who was to appear at later festivals as a short story writer and poet, sums it up:

> I remember the book festival in the College of Ripon and York St John. Jackie, my partner, was already using a small motorised wheelchair, and we had some difficulty getting it over bumps and thresholds. That may have been the year we ate one night in High Petergate, the small machine lumbering along the uneven pavement, and the Minster nearby brilliant under the floodlighting. The evening was an image of our lives at that time: the good food, the warmth of the restaurant, the exhilarating sense of friendship and of a larger community, were pleasures that absorbed and weren't yet distorted by the pressures of Jackie's disability. I think a lot of women there felt both validated and liberated by the sense of being

Christine Webb (far left) on an author panel the following year with Frances Gapper, Helen Sandler, Louise Tondeur (KW)

in an entirely accepting world, one in which they didn't have to explain themselves. We felt that too.

Even before the 2001 festival was over, Jenny was already envisioning the next step, promising readers of *Dykelife* – and especially those who had failed to get tickets this time – an 'even bigger celebration of lesbian writing' the following year.

Helen Sandler sees this period as a special moment in the history of lesbian publishing, which she experienced as both editor and writer:

> My short story from the first Diva anthology grew into a novel, *The Touch Typist*, so I was part of this list of new authors that we were developing at Diva Books, targeting a mainly lesbian audience. And behind it we had the might of *Diva* magazine: Gillian Rodgerson was the editor then, Kim Watson was a director, lots of knowledge of the market. At the same time Jenny had set up Libertas! and was finding lesbian books were selling really well. There turned out to be a big readership so it was a nice synergy. Jenny had really dynamic ideas for putting on events, where she would get audiences of hundreds – and eventually, thousands. So, the start of my involvement was at this exciting time, which I look back on now as quite a heyday of new lesbian books, of British lesbian imprints, and new authors who were excited to meet their readers. It felt as if things were on the up.

Despite this sense of optimism in the publishing world, life as a lesbian bookseller was far from easy. Even with the help of the wonderful book festival, Libertas! was struggling to make a profit. Times were hard for the book trade generally, and especially for women's books. In particular, the ending of the Net Book Agreement meant that a book no longer had an agreed cover price, and so could be sold at a discount. Big chains and supermarkets were able to offer huge discounts;

Diva books on offer at a later festival (LC)

small booksellers could not afford to compete.

In her memoir *A Bookshop of One's Own* (2024), Jane Cholmeley, one of the founders of the iconic Silver Moon bookshop in London's Charing Cross Road, describes in heartbreaking detail the struggle that small independent booksellers faced at that time. On one occasion, she writes, they discovered that Tesco was selling a book at a

Jenny Roberts in the bookshop

retail price below what it cost Silver Moon to buy it from the publisher. With the arrival of big chain bookstores and the growth of online shopping, the writing was on the wall for the independents. In fact, only a few weeks before the Libertas! Lesbian Book Festival in 2001, Silver Moon closed after seventeen glorious years: Libertas! was now the only women's bookshop in the country. Jenny saluted Silver Moon's achievement in *Dykelife*:

> We have never looked on Silver Moon as merely a competitor. We have always respected Jane and Sue for the commitment and hard work which, over seventeen years, has made them so special in the lesbian and feminist world. Also, right from the beginning, they have always been helpful and kind to us at Libertas!
>
> There should be room for all of us but, over the last few years, the remorseless march of the conglomerate bookshops (and one loss-making, price-cutting cyber-business in particular) has also seen the closure of alternative bookshops in Scotland, Manchester, Nottingham, Brighton and Hull.
>
> So we are genuinely saddened that Silver Moon will no longer be serving the community alongside us. Their loss is our loss too.

Some of the challenges Jenny had to face at this time were more personal. Later that year, Libertas! took a stall at the Saltaire Lesbian Christmas Fair in West Yorkshire. She recalls:

> It was a lovely affair, in this old hall in Saltaire. The organiser came and apologised to me that they'd been approached by a group from the Northern Older Lesbian Network, who thought that there should be a warning put up for people coming in, so they would know it wasn't entirely 'born women' in the hall.
> So, I had my customers coming up to me, saying, 'Jenny! Have you seen that notice in the entrance?'

It said something like, 'Caution! there is a transsexual in the room.' It was like I was a dangerous animal or something. It was quite amusing – most people were quite amused by it. And there were some who were quite upset that anybody would do that. But there were no bad effects on me at all – if anything, it reverberated on the people who insisted she put it up.

Counter-attack was never Jenny's style. Her attitude to being invited into women's space had always been that it was 'a privilege to be earned, rather than a right to be demanded'. The following year, NOLN asked if they could come to the book festival and give out leaflets to try and recruit new members.

I said, 'Yes, of course you can. You're very welcome.' And when they were there, I talked to them and made them feel welcome. That was what I did. I wasn't interested in conflict. I was much more interested in just getting on with people. It's worked quite well for me over the years, and I have managed to get on eventually even with those who were opposed to trans people. It's quite difficult to resist somebody who's not getting into conflict, and is being friendly. Why can't we all be like that?

The foundations Jenny laid are remembered with admiration and gratitude by many of the women who contacted me when this book was being written. Julie Fish, who went with friends to the York Lesbian Arts Festival sometime in the mid-2000s, spoke for many when she said:

I'm really grateful for the work that Jenny did in building inclusivity, her politics and her endeavours in lesbian, bisexual and queer women's communities. She wrote a reflective piece in *Diva* magazine around this time, about some of the potential tensions in LGBTQ communities. I saw her once at Brighton Pride, giving out leaflets about YLAF, and thanked her for her work. When we hear about events like Michigan Women's Festival, which was closed because of irreconcilable issues between queer women, we also need to remember that in the UK this was not our history. Instead, we have a proud history of queer women working together on a key LBQ women's event. ∎

Browsing through books and DVDs (LC)

It All Started in York
Lynne Calvert and Viviana Archer-Todde

LYNNE: Aww, wonderful YLAF! Viviana and I went to every single one, and it was terrific. Viviana had seen the festival advertised in *Shout* (a monthly magazine distributed throughout Yorkshire) and, being a wonderful bookworm, she really wanted to visit the festival.

VIVIANA: Well, I hardly drink, and pubs are not my thing, especially full of drunk women. And I adore books and reading. I assumed that if all the women were like me, it would be a better experience. I was truly excited to go!

LYNNE: I was more reluctant, but I agreed to be dragged along, and I'm so glad I did! We loved the fact it was here, up north, when so many big events were London-based. A huge part of needing to support this event was the fact that it wasn't held down south. To have such an event in York was just amazing. It was a small event, at St John's College. But after that, we went to them every year for the next however many years, right up to when, sadly, it folded – and it was fantastic!

VIVIANA: It was on 16 November 2001, at the festival, that my lovely Lynne proposed to me, before we went to the dance, and before we ate at Café Concerto, opposite the Minster. We must have been glowing, as the waiter said to us, 'I'm assuming we're celebrating?' We confirmed it, but didn't mention why or what. Shortly after, he brought an ice

FESTIVAL STORY

Lynne (left) and Viviana at their commitment ceremony

bucket with some fizz, and wished us congratulations! I felt in my heart that he knew, and we had that secret understanding between us that all LGBTQQI people have.

We had a commitment ceremony two years later in 2003, which was legally confirmed on 21 December 2005 when it became possible to have a civil partnership; and we were the first female couple in the borough of Bradford to be legally hitched. Then on 16 December 2014, again at nine in the morning, we were the first couple in Bradford to convert our civil partnership to a marriage.

But it all started in York. ∎

Linda Innes, ready to sign copies of her novel *Smother*, York Racecourse, 2002 *(KW)*

LESBIAN PRIDE AT THE RACECOURSE

THE LESBIAN BOOK FESTIVAL had been so successful, and there was so clearly an audience for such events, that the temptation to 'go larger' in 2002 was irresistible. Jenny remembers:

> The women were hungry for something that was theirs. Something that was good, and relaxed, and social, and *normal*. There wasn't much of that around in those days, was there? You met in back rooms of pubs, and often the surroundings were grotty and make-do. And what I wanted to do was to bring it right out into the open, and make it acceptable, and beautiful, and fun.

As soon as the Lesbian Book Festival at St John's was over, Jenny had opened negotiations with two of York's largest and most prestigious venues: the Racecourse and the Barbican Theatre. The bottom line, of course, was that she needed to sell books to keep Libertas! in business, and a big event like this would be a wonderful way of selling a lot of books in a short time. An ambitious number of tickets for this 'Lesbian Pride Weekend' (including 1200 for the book festival and 1500 for the concert at the Barbican) went on sale on 1 March 2002 – and quickly sold out. But it was still a calculated risk: if the weekend didn't turn a profit, Jenny would have to meet any shortfall out of her own savings.

So the horde of excited lesbian and bi women invading York that autumn found themselves in upgraded surroundings. Margaret Bird, who had attended the events at St John's, remembers the change of venue: 'The Racecourse was a big, bold place to have a lesbian event. It felt much more publicly visible – the festival was gaining confidence.' She adds, 'I felt an increased positive visibility around the city when travelling to YLAF. We were claiming our rights to have events just for us. These spaces are so precious, and easily marginalised.'

Val McDermid also remembers the move as ground-breaking:

> Going to the Racecourse was just amazing. Jenny was absolutely committed to excellent venues for women, and the Racecourse was a top-end venue. And it was quite astonishing to walk into those spaces, normally filled with gammons in suits and women in fancy hats, to see a bunch of lesbians of all shapes sizes and colours, rejoicing at the company they were in. It felt really subversive. It felt like, 'We're here and we're going to make changes. We're going to make things different.'

Proceedings opened at lunchtime on Friday 8 November with a public event at York Library. Jenny read from *Needle Point*; Stella Duffy read from her story 'Martha Gracc', which had just won a CWA Dagger; and Manda Scott (arriving just in time after a grim journey from Glasgow through storm and tempest) read from her soon-to-be-published novel, *Boudica: Dreaming the Eagle*, which would prove to be the start of a bestselling series.

That evening, the festival proper opened with the Diva Party Night, a social event for over a thousand women and the first of the many memorable lesbian occasions that would take place at York Racecourse from then on. Hilary Nowell, already a keen attendee at Libertas! events, expresses what many felt:

> I really thought we'd 'got there' when we started going to the Racecourse! I'm sure everybody did. And the banner, right across the entrance! It looked so good, didn't it?

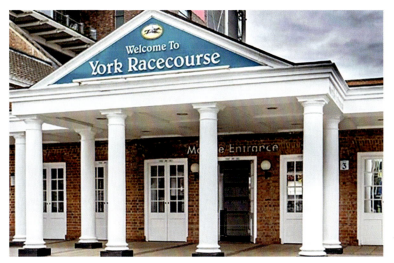

York Racecourse offered the biggest conference centre in the city

All the rooms and spaces at the venue had been renamed for the occasion, so that the screening of the film *Chutney Popcorn* took place in 'Rubyfruit Jungle', and the Showtime Concert in 'Radclyffe Hall', a big space on the ground floor. Organised and compered by singer-songwriter Claire Mooney, who performed tracks from her recently released album *Ordinary Rebel*, this concert included Rosie Lugosi the Lesbian Vampire; Clare Summerskill 'the lesbian Victoria Wood'; and the singer Belinda O'Hooley, in those days still a solo act.

On Saturday, the Racecourse was again the venue for the core event of the weekend, the much-loved Book Festival. It began with Ann Kaloski interviewing Sarah Waters in front of an adoring audience of over a thousand women. The adaptation of Sarah's debut novel *Tipping the Velvet* had just aired on BBC television. That rip-roaring picaresque tale, published by Virago in 1998 after multiple rejections, and the drama series that showed it all – from male impersonators belting out daring numbers in the Victorian music hall to raunchy sexual

LIBERTAS! LESBIAN BOOK
York Racecourse Centre · Saturda[y]
Programr[ne]

To avoid disappointment, please take your seats early
Seating in each room is limited and standing cannot be

Time	Radclyffe Hall	Ruby Fruit Jungle
9.30 am to 10.10 am	**Welcome** - Jenny Roberts followed immediately by... **Wordsmith** Ann Kaloski chats to **Sarah Waters** about her work	
10.30 am to 11.30 am	**First Kill Your Victim** *The rudiments of crime writing* Jay Taverner (Jane) investigates **Manda Scott**, **Elizabeth Woodcraft**, **Helen Shacklady** and **Virginia Smith**	**A Question of Character** *How real are the people in your book?* Amanda Boulter asks **Alma Fritchley**, **Eleanor Hill**, **Charlotte Mendelson** and **Jenny Roberts**
11.45 am to 12.30 pm		**Red Hot Writing** Kathleen Kiirik Bryson introduces excerpts from the *Red Hot Diva Collection* with readings from **Charlotte Cooper**, **Astrid Fox** and **Crin Claxton**
12.45 pm to 1.45 pm	**Any Questions?** *Ask anything you like!* Elizabeth Woodcraft puts your questions to **Manda Scott**, **Ali Smith**, **Charlotte Mendelson** and **Kathleen Kiirik Bryson**	**Never Let the Truth Get in the Way** *Is accuracy possible (or desirable) in historical fiction?* Helen Sandler quizzes **Sarah Waters**, **Alma Fritchley**, **Jay Taverner** and **Ellen Galford**
2.00 pm to 2.45 pm		**Women in Shorts - City Secrets** Cathy Bolton introduces excerpts from the new City Secrets anthology with contributions from **Rosie Lugosi**, **Jenny Roberts**, and **Susannah Marshall**
3.00 pm to 4.00 pm	**Any Questions?** *Ask anything you like!* Ellen Galford puts your questions to **Sarah Waters**, **Stella Duffy**, **Rose Collis** and **Helen Shacklady**	**Mind Your Language** *Are plot and character more important than use of English?* Manda Scott chews the syntax with **Ali Smith**, **Jay Taverner**(Jacky), **Eleanor Hill** and **Erica Wooff**
4.20 pm to 5.30 pm	**Closing Remarks** - Jenny Roberts followed immediately by... **Sandi Toksvig - Solo** Please do not take photographs during Sandi's Performance	
5.30 pm	Ends	Ends

Workshops are held on the Fourth Floor (turn right when you go through the double doors and walk to the far e[nd]

Floor Plan
A detailed plan of the Racecourse Centre can be found on page 17

FESTIVAL 2002
9th November 2002

IF YOU WISH TO SEE A PARTICULAR PANEL.
ALLOWED (EXCEPT FOR THE FINAL SESSION)

STONER'S LAIR	WOOLF DEN
TICKLE MY RIBS *The serious business of writing humour* Stephanie Theobald laughs out loud with VG Lee, Ellen Galford, Linda Innes and Jane Marlow **WOMEN IN SHORTS - LONG JOURNEY HOME** Caeia March introduces excerpts from the Long Journey Home anthology with contributions from **Frances Bingham, Julie Clare** and **Jocelyn Watson** **WRITE-ON DYKES** *Lesbian writer? Or a writer who happens to be lesbian?* Erica Wooff asks the question of **Stella Duffy, Stephanie Theobald, Jane Fletcher** and **Amanda Boulter** **SEX AND THE SINGLE WRITER** *Writing erotic interludes* Linda Innes gets fresh with **Stephanie Theobald, Charlotte Cooper, Virginia Smith** and **Crin Claxton** Ends	**WOMEN IN SHORTS - GROUNDSWELL** *Readings from the new Diva anthology* Helen Sandler introduces contributions from **Clare Summerskill, Kathleen Kiirik Bryson, Frances Gapper, Christine Webb** and **Louise Tondeur** **A QUESTION OF CHARACTER** *How real are the people in your book?* Crin Claxton puts the question to **Caeia March, Linda Innes, Frances Gapper** and **Jane Marlow** **DON WE NOW OUR GAY APPAREL** *Undressing Lesbian Lives* Rose Collis and Frances Bingham read and discuss their biographies of *Colonel Barker* and *Valentine Ackland* **PUBLISH AND BE DAMNED** *The mechanics of getting into print* Jay Taverner (Jane) turns the pages with **Lilian Mohin, Helen Sandler, Ann Kaloski** and **Jane Fletcher** Ends

nd of the passage). **PLEASE NOTE: These are only available to those who have pre-booked.**

FIRST AID is available by the cloakroom on the 3rd Floor. Qualified first aiders are on hand

A FREE CLOAKROOM is available on the third floor.

MOST TOILETS are designated for female use. However there is one toilet on the 3rd Floor which is reserved for male helpers

ING is
llowed in
art of the
ig
PT....
ightwood
nd Floor)
art of the
d Floor
ria on Sat

> *Interpreters*
> A signer is in attendance
> in Radclyffe Hall
> throughout the day.

encounters between women – were milestones for lesbian culture. Sarah was also promoting her award-winning new gothic novel, *Fingersmith*, and she was the star of that year's gathering. Jenny recalls:

> We had to give Sarah Waters protection from the hordes of women who wanted to be with her! If she walked anywhere, she was mobbed. In a very nice way, of course – it wasn't ever dangerous – but we had to shepherd her on and off the stage. Because the women there were just completely in thrall to her. She was a real star. It never really happened again with anybody else to the same extent.

Sarah herself remembers vividly the contrast between this festival and the first one she attended:

> I can't remember being invited to the first one. I just remember being there. I was newly single after a couple of longish relationships and I remember feeling a little bit on my own. At that point I'd just had the two books out, and still felt like a very young author.
>
> Then *Fingersmith* came out early in 2002 and also, crucially, *Tipping the Velvet* had been on telly only a few weeks before. So the difference of going to that second festival! I had another girlfriend by then. It was very early in our relationship, and she remembers that, as well – that I got a lot of lesbian love.
>
> It felt a bit overwhelming, but in a good way: it wasn't at all negative. I did an onstage interview in a big hall, and I remember a really big crowd. So, very different from my previous event, an author panel in a small room. There was lots of excitement, particularly about *Tipping the Velvet*, and then there were long lines of people wanting to have their books signed afterwards. I remember getting very hungry, and Stella Duffy appearing from nowhere, like a goddess, with a sandwich.

Sarah Waters (right) with partner Lucy (KW)

As well as having their books signed, people asked to have DVD covers signed, or to take pictures. Everyone takes pictures now, of course, but that felt like a change: 'Ooh, this is all a bit new!' But it was just really, really positive.

For the rest of the day, a variety of panels ran concurrently in four rooms (including 'Stoner's Lair' and 'Woolf Den'). As well as the familiar author readings, there was a very well-attended discussion called 'Publish and be Damned', where a panel of speakers with diverse publishing experience talked about the challenges of getting into print. One of them was the veteran lesbian publisher Lilian Mohin, director of Onlywomen Press, the ground-breaking lesbian feminist imprint founded in 1974. At question time, a member of the audience rose and made a moving impromptu tribute to Lilian, thanking her for her historic contribution to lesbian life.

In all, more than thirty authors read, chatted and signed books. While many were well known in the mainstream, or in the lesbian world, others were just starting out.

Among the debut authors was Crin Claxton – later to be festival director – with her first vampire novel, *Scarlet Thirst*, published by the spicy new Red Hot Diva imprint. Crin was deeply impressed by the whole experience:

> My socks were blown off, basically. Being at the festival and reading, getting feedback from readers, and just the mind-blowingly huge nature of the event, was amazing. But also, what was so wonderful was all the author chats at the hotel. At breakfast, or in the bar in the evening, or after events had finished, I just talked to so many different people. And everyone – the top authors, the well-known authors, Val and Manda and Stella – were all so approachable. I knew Stella Duffy anyway, because we had worked in theatre together, but I felt that everyone just rubbed along and was lovely. Just lovely to each other.

This egalitarian mix of famous authors with less well-known writers was a hallmark of the festivals. Christine Webb remembers: 'I had written a short story for the Diva anthology *Groundswell* and was delighted to appear in the same pages as Ali Smith and Jackie Kay.' (To her further delight, Ali was at the festival that year with a new novel, *Hotel World*, which had been shortlisted for both the Booker and Orange Prizes.) Christine gave a reading with other authors from the anthology: Clare Summerskill, Kathleen Kiirik Bryson, Frances Gapper and Louise Tondeur. She says:

> Short stories aren't my thing, but this one grew out of my mind quite simply, and its central figure surfaced from I don't know where. I could see her quite plainly: rather heavy-set, the face reserved, impassive, used to concealing emotion. It was some time before I noticed her artificial leg. At the festival I got the chance to introduce her to an audience. It was great fun.

Laka Daisical and Deirdre Cartwright of The Electric Landladies (KW)

The Book Festival closed with a hilarious solo performance by returning favourite Sandi Toksvig, and Lesbian Pride Weekend came to a triumphant conclusion that evening with the Libertas! Celebration Concert at the 1500-seat Barbican Concert Hall. Billed as 'one of the biggest lesbian concerts ever staged in the North', it was produced and directed by Jean T and compered by Julie McNamara. The acts included Martha and Eve (the artists formerly known as Donna and Kebab), the Electric Landladies band, comedian Rhona Cameron and singer Horse.

Horse remembers that she was quite ill at the time, but was determined to go on:

> I'd done the sound check, and I was sweating and couldn't breathe properly. (I'd been seriously ill some time before that, while on tour, and never completely recovered.) I was lying on a chaise longue in the dressing room, and Rhona Cameron came in.

> She said, 'What the fuck's wrong with you?'
> And I just gasped. Couldn't speak.
> Then she said, 'You've got asthma. Get to hospital or you'll die!'
> She has asthma herself, and she knew. I had no idea that was what was wrong with me! I was taken to the nearest hospital, and I was nebulised for over four hours. I came straight back from that, got onstage and performed; then I went out to face 3000 lesbians, signing stuff for people, and was absolutely *engulfed* – I'd forgotten how crazy it can be. Such a buzz. I eventually had to stop and was taken away, because the effects of the nebulisation had worn off – I was breathless once more.
> But of course I went back again for more the next year!

The concert was a memorable close to a wonderful weekend. But, in spite of the festival's resounding success, the last women's bookshop in the UK was still struggling to break even. In an attempt to reduce costs, Libertas! had relocated the previous year to smaller premises at 50 Fossgate. It had outlasted many other small independent bookshops, but ultimately could not escape their fate. The business was still making a loss and it was clear to Jenny and Ann that something radical had to be done. Sadly, they made the decision that Libertas! would have to close – but not until they had staged one last, magnificent event. Although she was already hosting the biggest gathering in the UK's lesbian calendar, Jenny was determined that her final festival would be bigger and better still. Libertas! was about to go international. ∎

Queuing to have books signed by (from top): Sandi Toksvig *(LC)*, Jane Marlow and Ali Smith *(KW)*, Stephanie Theobald *(KW)*

The Celebration Concert finale featured The Electric Landladies, Martha and Eve, Jean T, Horse, Rhona Cameron and Julie McNamara, joined onstage by authors and organisers
(Caroline Clark)

An Impertinent Question
Hilary Nowell

Pauline (left) and Hilary (right) with Jane Hoy at the festival *(HS)*

I think we went to the very first book festival, at St John's. It was exciting to be going somewhere where everyone was like us. By that time, we'd been together about thirty years, but we knew no-one else like us – not a soul. So it was all quite new to us: we'd never done anything like this before. We were already in our early sixties. We wondered if we were too old!

Pauline didn't want to go, at first. She was afraid she might see someone that might know her. And I said, 'Well, they might be equally reluctant to be recognised!' That was always the fear, though, wasn't it?

As the festival got bigger and went to the Racecourse, they would put different events on, too. You could go to the cinema: they put special films on. That was magic to us – to be able to go into a cinema and watch the kind of films we could enjoy. And I liked it because you could sit and hold hands, and feel OK about it – there was nowhere else you could do that. And to have got to the ages that we had... it was lovely.

The atmosphere was brilliant. Everybody was so friendly; you'd be talking away to people you'd never met before. It was a real buzz. Nothing, absolutely nothing was going to blank that weekend out – we were definitely going to it! It was just special. We couldn't wait – we were marking it off on the calendar! Exciting times for us.

FESTIVAL STORY

As soon as you got your programme, you marked it, and it was 'how could you get to them all?' Going from room to room and lift to lift, and managing to eat as well (though the food came second in importance). The part that I enjoyed the most was when the authors read to you, and then when you took it home and read the book, you could still hear their voices.

It was always interesting to see the queues for the signings afterwards, and it was lovely to talk to the authors. As you went more regularly, there was a familiarity, so we were able to take quite a few books that we'd bought before, to be signed by them.

Going to the Racecourse for the disco, we'd have a taxi, because then you could have a drink and relax. But saying to the taxi driver to drop us at the Racecourse, and the banners were all across saying 'YLAF' and 'Lesbian Arts' and all that… Oh, we felt on show, to be going there like that.

It was at a disco that one young lady knelt down at the side of us and asked an impertinent question (but she didn't think it was). There were all these young ones – students, I should think, some of them – and we had a conversation, and then one of them said, 'Do you mind if I ask you a question?'

So I said, 'No of course not.'

And she said, 'Do you still… do it?'

Well! What do you say? Do you tell the truth? Or do you say, 'No comment'? So I said to them, 'Of course! Why not? Does it ever stop?'

We must have seemed very old to them.

They were magical times, actually. The happiest of memories. A big part of our life, at that time. To be able to celebrate your relationship, and feel that you could be like that in public! And as the younger people came along, which they did as it continued, they were there with a different attitude. Because they were beginning to be used to being free. ■

The rising threat of online shopping, as charted by Alison Bechdel

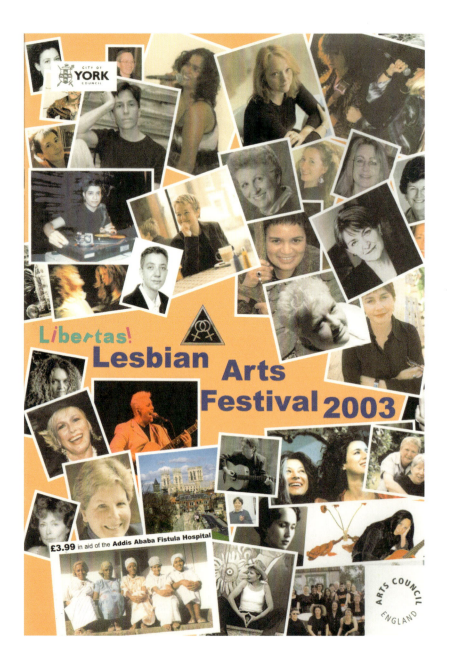

A CELEBRATION LIKE NEVER BEFORE

Jenny was determined that the Libertas! story would end with a bang rather than a whimper and this last festival would be 'a celebration, the like of which has never been seen before'. The change of name from 'book festival' to 'arts festival' had been voted for by those attending the previous year, and indicated how far the occasion had grown beyond being just a literary event. Many of the other additions or tweaks to the programme were also in response to audience feedback. Extending over five days, in a dozen venues across the city of York, the Libertas! Lesbian Arts Festival offered more than ever.

Audience member Lisa Hinkins summed up the uniqueness of the festival:

> I remember thinking it was great that it was somewhere like York, where you wouldn't necessarily think this kind of festival would be, and that actually it was quite fitting for such a historic place. The fact that there was this women's bookshop was amazing, and that it was a books festival, with a proper cultural basis – as opposed to just necking a few beers in a nightclub and having a disco. It was tapping into something that hadn't been explored before: lesbian literature and the arts, something quite hidden – niche – so you had to really try and find it.

It felt important enough for Lisa and her partner to travel all the way from Brighton. The story she told me also captures the speed with which the festival had grown:

> I do remember the first time we went. We just got tickets for the day, and incorporated it in a long weekend. We

really enjoyed it. Then we decided to go the following year, and we might have done two days, and then the third time (which was the last year Jenny was running it) we took the week off, and we went up there and I think we booked something for every one of the five days of the festival!

An event of this size and complexity was already an extraordinary achievement for the Libertas! team, especially as most of them were volunteers. To grow further, it needed a firmer financial foundation. Jenny had realised at an early stage that to mount the festival she wanted for 2003 she would have to find an additional source of funding. Authors had always participated for free, or for nominal expenses, in the hope of selling their books; but musical performers had to be paid, as did the BSL signers and the bus company putting on a special service to and from the Racecourse. The main venues were expensive; so were lighting and sound systems and overnight accommodation for authors and performers. This

A typical packed audience at the Racecourse (LC)

year, there would also be writers from the across the world with substantial fares to pay. All this meant another huge hike in the cost of putting on the festival. There was a limit to how far ticket prices could be increased, and Jenny wanted to keep the event affordable. A bid for Arts Council funding had been the obvious next step.

The success of such a bid was in no way guaranteed. As Helen Sandler explained to me:

> The difficulty you had at that time was that the Arts Council had no priority for doing lesbian or gay events. It was seen as an obscure minority – they didn't understand it as a marginalised group that needed help.

This was the barrier Jenny had to break through. She couldn't delay hiring venues or booking acts until the result of the bid was known, so she and the team began to put the festival together regardless, advertising it in *Dykelife* and even beginning to sell tickets. It wasn't until July, when planning was already at an advanced stage and ticket sales were taking off, that confirmation of an Arts Council grant finally came through, to everyone's huge relief. Libertas! was now recognised and supported both by York City Council and by a major national funding body, putting lesbian writing and performance on the cultural map in a whole new way. A celebratory front-page article in *Dykelife* described the difference the money would make, and reflected that this was also a triumph in terms of the public perception of lesbian life:

> We feel very much that we are making a difference […] and, between us, we are turning a small alternative festival into something which is playing its part in changing the society in which we live.

This year, the festival aimed to make a wider difference, too:

Singer Aneesa Chaudhry (LC)

all proceeds from the sale of the souvenir programme went directly to Ethiopaid, to support the women's Fistula Hospital in Addis Ababa.

The Libertas! Lesbian Arts Festival of 2003 was the stuff of legend. It took place from 29 October to 2 November, in the week of the autumn half-term holiday. For festival-goers who could arrive in York as early as Wednesday, there were writing workshops with favourites such as VG Lee and Elizabeth Woodcraft, and a performance of Julie McNamara's solo show *Pig Tales*. On the Thursday, Jackie Kay and Stella Duffy also ran writing workshops; there were two guided walks though York's historic 'snickleways' and another film screening, before the All-Star Concert at the Barbican. Once again, Jean T was the show's producer; Sandi Toksvig compered. The bill spanned decades of lesbian performance, from veteran folk singer Julie Felix to contemporary favourite Horse.

A very young Aneesa Chaudhry was a memorable support act. Now a successful jazz-singer and voice coach, she giggled as she told me:

> As the newcomer onstage that night, I was really nervous about supporting big name acts like Julie Felix and Horse. It was in my very early days of performing, and I think I got a bit over-excited, because when I sang 'I Just Wanna Make Love to You', I lap-danced Sandi Toksvig.

Sandi made a rapid recovery from this unrehearsed bit of stage business:

> She went along with it, but then called my bluff, by picking me up and dancing me around the stage. The howling and laughing from the audience was blooming brilliant.

Lisa Hinkins was in the audience, and remembers it vividly:

We had really good seats, only a few rows from the front. Aneesa Chaudhry was brilliant, and then Sandi Toksvig came onstage to thank her or something, and the next minute Aneesa was lap-dancing her. And I swear Sandi Toksvig went as red as a beetroot.

For Lisa, looking back now, the moment was not just gloriously funny, but politically significant:

> I thought it was great that there were women, onstage, having permission to do that. Because it would have been highly unusual for that to be seen in a venue like that, in York. And also, that the place had almost sold out – fairly sizeable venue, that.

The Book Festival that started next morning was bigger than ever. It had expanded to two days and for the first time featured international as well as British writers, with some of the biggest names coming from the USA. These included Katherine V Forrest, the prolific, multi-award-winning Canadian/American author of lesbian classics such as *Curious Wine*, *Daughters of a Coral Dawn* and the Kate Delafield detective series. Other authors, as well as audience members, were excited at the prospect of meeting this lesbian icon. Val McDermid told me:

> There was a sense of excitement about meeting people whose books you'd read, but you'd never met them before. And particularly that was the case with the Americans, when they came over – people like Katherine Forrest – it was meeting your heroes.

The feeling was reciprocated. Katherine remembers the Libertas! Lesbian Arts Festival as 'an unforgettable event in my life', saying:

> My overriding memory is the sheer exhilaration of being there with the three indisputable queens of British fiction,

who'd given us novels I knew would be part of our permanent literature. Val McDermid, with her incredible body of work, and her recent *A Place of Execution*, which I rank in the very top tier of our best-ever mystery fiction. Manda Scott, with the brilliant *Boudica* series. Sarah Waters, already world-famous with her *Tipping the Velvet* and *Fingersmith*.

I remember being on a panel with Val, and our mind-matching over what was crucial to both of us in maintaining the integrity in our mystery series; I remember sitting at a table signing books, amid a world of lesbian writers, with these illustrious queens around me; I remember the audiences packing the rooms for the panels, many of them women of academic achievement from all over Europe, and feeling so proud of the extraordinary range of our lesbian community.

Alongside her writing, Katherine V Forrest had for ten years been editor of Naiad Press, the world's oldest and longest-lasting lesbian publisher. A generation older than most of her audience, she spoke passionately about lesbian culture and community. Her assertion that 'coming out is the unfinished business on our community's agenda' struck a chord with many of her listeners, for whom the festival was a rare space of freedom in a closeted life. Even though, in the UK, Section 28 had been repealed earlier that year, fear and hiding were still the norm for many – perhaps most – lesbians at that time. For some, YLAF was an opportunity to think about being braver, to try out new ideas. Hilary Nowell, for instance, remembers that, 'Stella Duffy was the first person I ever heard say "my wife" – and I thought that was magic! It sounded so natural, as well, and we all wanted to say it.'

By contrast, Novelist Manda Scott remembers the confidence of the younger festival-goers:

> The thing that really stood out – and still stands out for me – was watching crowds of *young* women, going round

Book Festival Programme ~ Friday 31ˢᵗ October

TIME	EVENT	PLACE
9.00am to 9.45am	**Dying for Breakfast** - **Katherine V Forrest** and **Claire McNab** in early morning conversation about murder and mayhem	RADCLYFFE
10.00 am to 11.00 am 4 panels to choose from	**Lesbian/Feminist Issues Worldwide** - the differences, both in and out of print **Ann Kaloski** talks with **Inga Muscio, Karin Meissenburg, Lauren Maddison** and **Eleanor Hill**	WOOLF
	Funny HA HA! - the serious business of writing humour **Crin Claxton** laughs out loud with **VG Lee, Amanda Boulter, Alison Bechdel** and **Kay Vale**	RADCLYFFE
	Literal Choice - authors discuss books that defy genre **Ellen Galford** quizzes **Charlotte Mendelson, Louise Tondeur, Stella Duffy** and **Stephanie Theobald**	STONER'S
	From Lindsay with Love - **Val McDermid** launches **Hostage to Murder** The 6th, long-awaited **Lindsay Gordon** mystery - published today by Harper Collins	RUBY FRUIT
11.15am to 12 noon	**Work-in-Progress** - **Sarah Waters** reads from the novel which she is currently writing - set in 1940's London - and talks about her work.	RADCLYFFE
12.15 pm to 1.15 pm 4 panels to choose from	**Queer Family** - writing it, thinking it, living it **Amanda Boulter** questions the differences with **Cathie Dunsford, Stella Duffy, Helen Larder, Louise Tondeur**	WOOLF
	Delightfully Dead - Introducing Necrologue, the brand new DIVA anthology **Helen Sandler** introduces readings from **Ellen Galford, Elizabeth Woodcraft, VG Lee** and **Robyn Vinten**	RADCLYFFE
	Any Questions - authors talk about world events and trivia **Jay Taverner (Jacky)** puts the topics to **Helen Shacklady, Charlotte Mendelson, Elizabeth Lewis** and **Jill Gardiner**	STONER'S
	The Warrior Queen - **Manda Scott** reads and talks about the research, the dedication and the joy that is going into the writing of her highly acclaimed four-part epic on the life and times of **Boudica** the first Queen of all England.	RUBY FRUIT
1.30 pm to 2.15 pm 2 events to choose from	**Mystery Fiction and the Divine Feminine** - **Lauren Maddison** tells all	RUBY FRUIT
	More Soap from Balham - **Amanda Boulter** launches **Back Around the Houses** Even more hilarious 'tales of the city' from that very queer street in South London.	WOOLF
2.30 pm to 3.30 pm 4 panels to choose from	**Desert Island of Lesvos** - What book would you take? **Crin Claxton** asks for explanations from **Elizabeth Woodcraft, Helen Shacklady, Elizabeth Lewis** and **Stephanie Theobald**	STONER'S
	Hearts & Flowers - the role of love and romance in lesbian fiction **Jay Taverner (Jacky)** pops the question to **Sarah Waters, Helen Larder, Eleanor Hill** and **Ruby Vise**	RUBY FRUIT
	Dead Good Women - the art of fictional killing and detection **Jay Taverner (Jane)** investigates with **Katherine V Forrest, Claire McNab, Jane Fletcher, Val McDermid**	RADCLYFFE
	Thinking in Pictures - visualising make believe worlds **Helen Sandler** takes a flight of fancy with **Manda Scott, Louise Tondeur, Charlotte Mendelson** and **Kay Vale**	WOOLF
3.45 pm to 4.30 pm 3 events to choose from	**Talking Cunt** - **Ann Kaloski** talks to **Inga Muscio** about her best selling, and immensely entertaining, womaniferto - **cunt: a declaration of independence**	WOOLF
	Song of the Selkies - **Cathie Dunsford's** magical readings from her eco-novels are interwoven with waiata (indigenous songs) and karanga (calls for action). Music especially composed for these performances is sung, and played on the clay-ocarina, by **Karin Meissenburg**	RUBY FRUIT
	Murder in a Woman's World - **Jane Fletcher** revisits **Celaeno's World** as she launches her exciting new mystery thriller **The Wrong Trail Knife**.	STONER'S
4.45pm to 5.45pm	**Alison Bechdel's Slide Show** **Helen Sandler** introduces an hour of slides and stories from the legendary artist of the **Dykes To Watch Out For** series.	RADCLYFFE

BOOK FESTIVAL PROGRAMME ~ SATURDAY 1ST NOVEMBER

TIME	EVENT	PLACE
9.00am to 9.45am	**Return to the Gateways Club** - Jay Taverner (Jane) talks to *Jill Gardiner* about her book on the legendary Lesbian Nightclub, and the women who went there	RADCLYFFE*
10.00 am to 11.00 am 4 panels to choose from	**Lesbian/Feminist Issues Worldwide** - the differences, both in and out of print Helen Sandler talks with *Stella Duffy, Cathie Dunsford, Elizabeth Woodcraft and Inga Muscio*	WOOLF
	Thinking in Pictures - visualising make-believe worlds VG Lee takes a flight of fancy with *Alison Bechdel, Helen Larder, Jane Fletcher and Ruby Vise*	RUBY FRUIT*
	Desert Island of Lesvos - What book would you take? Crin Claxton asks for explanations from *Louise Tondeur, Val McDermid, Helen Shacklady, Sarah Waters*	RADCLYFFE*
	Joined-up Writing - the process of writing, the joy of words Ellen Galford chews the syntax with *Lauren Maddison, Claire McNab, Amanda Boulter and Elizabeth Lewis*	STONER'S
11.15am to 12 noon	**An Audience With...** *Katherine V Forrest* and *Claire McNab* answer audience questions and talk to Jay Taverner (Jane) about their work.	RADCLYFFE*
	The Warrior Queen - *Manda Scott* reads and talks about the research, the dedication and the joy that is going into the writing of her highly acclaimed, four-part epic on the life and times of *Boudica* the first Queen of all England.	RUBY FRUIT
12.15 pm to 1.15 pm 4 panels to choose from	**Any Questions** - authors talk about world events and trivia Helen Sandler puts the topics to *Katherine V Forrest, Stella Duffy, Eleanor Hill*	RADCLYFFE*
	What's Hot? - Why are lesbians in fiction so damn sexy? And what is sexy anyway? Crin Claxton gets fresh with *Stephanie Theobald, Kay Vale, Ruby Vise and Jill Gardiner*	STONER'S
	Queer Family - writing it, thinking it, living it Ann Kaloski questions the differences with *Helen Larder, Inga Muscio, VG Lee*	WOOLF
	Dead Good Women - the art of fictional killing and detection Jay Taverner(Jacky) investigates with *Lauren Maddison, Elizabeth Woodcraft, Val McDermid and Helen Shacklady*	RUBY FRUIT*
1.30 pm to 2.15 pm 2 events to choose from	**More Soap from Balham** - *Amanda Boulter* launches *Back Around the Houses* Even more hilarious 'tales of the city' from that very queer street in South London.	RUBY FRUIT
	The Map of My Life - The Life Story of *Emma Humphries* is launched this week in a new book by the Justice for Women Campaign. All profits go to help other abused women get out of prison. Julie Bindel talks about the human consequences of a sometimes insensitive legal system. (Copies of the book will be available to buy)	RADCLYFFE
2.30 pm to 3.30 pm 4 panels to choose from	**Funny HA HA!** - The serious business of writing humour Elizabeth Woodcraft joins in the laughter with *VG Lee, Kay Vale and Stephanie Theobald*	WOOLF
	Hearts & Flowers - the role of love and romance in lesbian fiction Ann Kaloski goes all gooey with *Claire McNab, Eleanor Hill, Louise Tondeur and Elizabeth Lewis*	STONER'S
	From Lindsay with Love - *Val McDermid* launches *Hostage to Murder* The 6th, long-awaited *Lindsay Gordon* mystery - published yesterday	RUBY FRUIT*
	Another Time, Another Place - Historical Fiction vs Fantasy Fiction - What's the difference? Jay Taverner (Jacky) takes a trip with *Manda Scott, Jane Fletcher, Katherine V Forrest and Sarah Waters*	RADCLYFFE*
3.45 pm to 4.30 pm 3 events to choose from	**From Honor to Expletive** - *Inga Muscio* talks about the philosophy and the principles behind her controversial book - *cunt: a declaration of Independence*. Introduced by Ann Kaloski	RUBY FRUIT
	A Dyke to Watch Out For - Ellen Galford talks to *Alison Bechdel* about her life and work	RADCLYFFE*
	Getting Published: The Inside Story - *Cathie Dunsford* and *Karin Meisenburg* launch a new handbook for women writers which presents a much needed lesbian-feminist perspective on the publishing industry	WOOLF
4.45pm to 5.45pm	**Jackie Kay - in person** *Jackie Kay* talks about, and reads from, her work. Introduced by Helen Sandler	RADCLYFFE*

*Sign Language Interpreters present at these sessions

together, completely in their skin and happy; and thinking, 'There was nothing like this when I was that age.' I was always really heartened and impressed by their sense of self. It was just glorious.

And the fact that this thing existed, that they *could* turn up in a busload – there'd be groups of twenty or thirty going round together. It was so cool.

There were, clearly, older women too. There wasn't social media then, but we'd just hit a point when it was possible to get the word out to people who'd lived all their lives isolated – 'Hey, guys, you'll be amongst friends here!' And they could come, and it was amazing.

The fact that so many women *had* heard about the festival, without the kind of digital communication we take for granted now, was a testament to the networking that existed within the lesbian community at that time. Libertas! communicated

Above: Alison Bechdel signing books *(Jude Brett)*
Opposite (L to R): Jane Fletcher, Stella Duffy, Val McDermid, Manda Scott and Jane Traies on a panel in 2006 *(LC)*

with its customers through the available print media, *Dykelife* and *Diva* magazine; and then women told other women. And it worked: the number of tickets sold for the 2003 festival was nearly three thousand.

Alongside Katherine V Forrest, the other big name from the USA that year was Alison Bechdel, whose cartoon strip *Dykes to Watch Out For* ('part soap-opera and part op-ed column') was well-loved on both sides of the Atlantic. She had just published the tenth book in the series, *Dykes and Sundry Other Carbon-Based Life Forms to Watch Out For*; and entertained a packed hall for an hour, showing slides and talking about her work. Alison made a lasting impression on several of the people who shared their memories with me. Rachel Whitbread said:

> I was queueing for her book signing and, when I got to the front, I asked her for 'a tip of the nib'. (On the side of some

CELEBRATION CONCERT ~ PROGRAMME

Doors open 6.45 pm   Show Starts 8.00 pm   Show ends approx 11.00 pm   Late Bar (subject to licence)

Jean T presents...

The hilarious comedy duo

Chambers & Nettleton

who welcome...

Halcyon
'kicking folkie acoustic butt'

Rosie Wilby & Virginia MacNaughton

soft but gutsy
sultry & powerful
TWO singer/songwriters
ONE powerful duo

Interval
Approx 9.00 pm to 9.25pm

Martha & Eve
folk, rock, soul...
with a saucy twist of flamenco Mediterranean style!

Never the Bride
mixing bluesy, soulful heavy rock with emotive power ballads...

Please note that photography and recording are not allowed during the show
Programme subject to change

of her drawings, she writes, 'Tip o' the nib to...' and then names someone; it's like a salute or doffing of the cap, but with a pen... So, I wanted one of them.) And she said, no one had ever asked her for that before. I was so chuffed that I'd got the first 'tip of the nib'!

Helen Shacklady, novelist and later YLAF board member, reflected wryly that:

> YLAF has had a lasting influence on my life. Every time I hear the words 'Bechdel Test', I gnash my teeth. Because the year the great Alison Bechdel herself came to the festival, I found myself in a lift with her and – instead of me impressing her with insight, wit and pertinent questions about her seminal works – the conversation was about custard. I'm sure she remembers this as vividly as I do.

Nic Herriot interviewed Alison for *Diva* magazine:

> Never meet your heroes, they say, so I was a bit worried. But no. She was perfect. Absolutely. And I've kept bumping into her since – she sent me a book, and I previewed it; and then she sent me another one, and I did a review on the web. Things like that. So occasionally I've met Alison Bechdel in my life since – and never been let down. That's the one hero you can meet. She's brilliant.

In the resulting article, Nic reflected on the way in which *Dykes to Watch Out For* drew on real life: for instance, when the fictional women's bookstore Madwimmin is forced to close, losing out to larger global conglomerates. 'The recently announced closure of Libertas! itself came to mind as I read it,' Nic wrote.

On the Friday night of the festival, there was a second concert at the Barbican. Comedians Chambers and Nettleton compered, introducing the American folk duo Halcyon, performing for the first time in the UK; singer/songwriter Rosie Wilby; Martha and Eve; and the 'Queens of Blues Rock', Never the Bride. For festival-goers who still had the energy, there was a late-night screening of the moving documentary *Aimée and Jaguar*, too. This was part of a season of lesbian films that ran at City Screen, York's riverside cinema and café-bar, over the whole five days.

The second day of the book festival began with Jill Gardiner reading from her recently published history of the legendary Gateways Club, *From the Closet to the Screen*. She recorded her impressions of the day in her journal:

> Saturday 1 November. It has been a roller-coaster of emotion being here – sheer terror, excitement, that awful yearning to fit in and fear of not being accepted – and then a warm relaxed sensation when people, as some do, have responded to me in a friendly and warm way.
>
> It is a real revelation that Jackie Kay and Sarah Waters felt really nervous before reading. You wouldn't know. I love Stella Duffy's great honesty as well. She read a wonderful piece about the long process by which she first got published and overcame her sense that only posh people were allowed to write.
>
> It is quite bewildering meeting so many writers at once. It is great how equal it all is – all the writers get the same fee, stay in the same hotel, feel like equals in the sense that we are all here to participate in readings and panels…
>
> There has been a lot of interest in my book and it sold out by about 11 o'clock yesterday, within an hour of my reading. Most of the purchasers never went to the Gateways – they were all ages but there were a lot of young women, who felt, as Charlotte Mendelson put it in a panel we were both on, 'I wish I could have gone to the Gateways.' I wasn't mobbed but was steadily approached all day by women who'd read the book and loved it or were going to read it and were looking forward to it.

Writer Jill Gardiner

For the rest of the day, there were dozens of author panels and other events to choose from. Amanda Boulter launched her second book, *Back Around the Houses*; Jane Fletcher launched *The Wrong Trail Knife*; Manda Scott held the audience spellbound with readings and revelations about her *Boudica* series; and Sarah Waters read from her work in progress, the story which would become *The Night Watch*. The book festival ended with a lively reading by Jackie Kay. Then there was just time for music-lovers to take in a performance of *Patience and Sarah*, an opera based on Isabel Miller's classic historical novel of the same name, before the ever-popular women-only disco.

It was much appreciated that festival discos fell on the last Saturday in October, when the clocks go back, and everyone got an extra hour of dancing. The discos had always been a popular part of the festivals, but this one was particularly memorable.

Watching the street concert *(LC)*

It opened with the sound of the Scottish women's drumming band, SheBoom. Thirty drummers had travelled down from Glasgow for the weekend and the impact of their percussion, under the low ceiling at the Racecourse, was unforgettable. Clare Morris, who is still a member of SheBoom, told me:

> It was absolutely amazing. We were playing on the stage – well actually, in front of the stage because there were too many of us to be on the stage – and security guards came and linked arms to hold the crowd back, as all these women surged forward. I felt like a rock star!
>
> We're a women's band, so women's spaces are especially important to us. I've never been part of anything like YLAF before or since, and I think it should be obligatory that everyone gets to experience that. There should be central government funding for it!

Her friend and fellow-drummer Joyce Nicholson agreed:

> We've been to other women's festivals. We've played all over Europe. All sorts of amazing spaces. But there was something truly unique, I think, about the York Lesbian

Arts Festival. To have that many women in that space, doing lots of different things artistically – that was totally unique. Could it happen now? It should! It would be a very powerful thing to have a lesbian arts festival again.

On Sunday, for the first time (but not the last), the Lesbian Arts Festival moved out on to the streets of York. In the middle of Parliament Street, outside Marks and Spencer, a stage was erected for an outdoor concert. Jenny Roberts remembers that this innovation had been enthusiastically supported by York City Council:

> They said we had to wait till 12, till the churches finished, but then we were allowed to start. The Council were right behind it. Such a good council in York! They're so keen on getting people into the city.

Claire Mooney organised and compered this outdoor concert, as well as performing in it (at one point she had Jenny playing the kazoo – rather badly, according to the kazooist). Although

Claire Mooney (left) in 'a little takeover of York' *(Appature-Images)*

Claire organised the festival cabarets and many of the high-profile indoor concerts, too, she admitted:

> If I'm honest, that was my favourite, the outside gig. We made noise. We were seen. So important. Well, to me it was – I'm a political animal and this was about our visibility… a little takeover of York. It was always pouring down, but it was just brilliant! It was lovely, it was fun.
>
> The only hassle we got was from the people from the council – God bless them, got a job to do, I know – when people who performed tried to sell their CDs and hadn't got a licence. But that was the only issue.
>
> And truly, there was some atrocious weather and everything, but I thought it was amazing, that we could do that in the centre of York. It was just a real affirmation of us.

As well as the lesbian audience, many people out shopping in York stopped to watch and listen. Kate North, a York-based writer and later a member of the YLAF Board, observed:

> The normal street activity in the centre of York involves Vikings or Roman soldiers, or maybe the odd street artist doing clown work or being a statue. So to have scores, even hundreds of lesbians arrive on the main shopping street, to take part or watch the performers, was brilliant.

As the concert drew to its end, the surrounding buildings vibrated to the sound of SheBoom's drums. Joyce Nicholson remembers:

> Playing out on the street was different from the Racecourse – we managed to fit on the stage! It was quite a tight fit, when you're drumming with your arms flailing. We had to play neatly, which is not that usual. But we managed to do it, and nobody fell off.

Poet Christine Webb wasn't in the crowd, but couldn't miss the joyful noise:

I'd lost my driving glasses in the canteen after my reading, so I spent part of Saturday afternoon having an eye-test, then had to go back on Sunday morning to collect a new pair. While I waited for Specsavers to open, the massed drummers thundered in the street – a terrific sound and spectacle!

The drumming was, in Jenny's words, 'the last live performance of the final Libertas! Festival'. In just five years, the lesbian visibility she had dreamed of when she opened the bookshop had become a reality. As she wrote in that 2003 festival programme, 'Together, we have all made a political point which I hope, in some small way at least, will take us further along the road to equality and respect.' ■

The street concert became an institution *(A-I)*

SheBoom back by popular demand in 2005 *(LC)*

Silver Rings
Dawn and Louise Jutton

LOUISE: Living in the middle of nowhere, as we did, lesbian fiction was not on our radar. And it wasn't possible to just go into a bookshop and get this material – other than perhaps at Birmingham Pride, where you might see a couple of books for sale. So we would make this pilgrimage to York, where there was a sea of beige fleeces and sensible shoes – all the lesbians trotting off to Libertas! It was fantastic. And we would stock up with lesbian books for the year.

DAWN: I think that's what I remember most about it. It was like we suddenly *invaded* York... and I think the reason we kept going was that connection with so many women, who were all there for the same reason – because they loved books, and they wanted to be with other women who loved books. And of course, the fact that the great majority of them were gay. For us, being gay, loving books, loving York – it was just this magical concoction. We've never forgotten it.

LOUISE: Being able to talk to the authors of the books you'd been reading – that was fantastic, too. That first year, I bought a lot of Alma Fritchley's books. Most of them involved classic cars and, at the time, I had a Triumph GT6, and Dawn had a Spitfire. So I kind of shuffled up to Alma and said, 'I really enjoy your books and I've got a classic car as well...' That's how we started talking. Then she told me about how she wrote her books in her lunch hour at work. So we had a good chat with her. She still pops up now and then – sends us a message...

FESTIVAL STORY

Louise (left) and Dawn Jutton with Flynn on their wedding day

DAWN: The other thing YLAF gave us – as a couple who were living semi in the closet, because of family stuff – it gave a special element to our relationship. We already shared a love of literature, but going to those places was quite romantic. Because you suddenly felt comfortable and at ease in yourself, and not alone. You're in a place where your sexuality has no negative impact, you can suddenly be a person, with all that gone. And you're with other people who share a love of books and a love of music.

LOUISE: It was something totally different from our regular lives. We couldn't get there quick enough! And we'd come home with these *piles* of books that were supposedly going to last us all year, and we'd have read them all in a couple of months!

DAWN: In 2003, we walked around York and there, sitting in the front room of a little terraced house, was this guy making rings and things. A silversmith. Sitting in his shopfront. And we decided to have some rings made by him. This was even before civil partnerships. So we said, well, we can't get married, but we could still exchange rings. We'd only been together about five years, then.

LOUISE: We chatted to him and he said, 'Would you like to come in and finish making the rings?' So we both made each other's ring. I can even remember what music was playing – Coldplay's 'Clocks' on his CD player – and we sat at this little machine finishing off these silver rings he'd made.

DAWN: Then we just went upstairs in our rented house when our friends were out, had a cuddle, and swapped these rings. It was our own little commitment ceremony. And when we had our civil partnership in Brighton, we'd already got the rings, so we used them then. We ran away to Brighton to have a really quiet civil partnership. So when we actually got married – converted our partnership – we decided to celebrate that with something that actually looked like a wedding. And we used these rings again.

LOUISE: We went to York again only last year, but we couldn't find the shop. I don't think he was still there.

DAWN: In the context of our relationship, as a newish couple who had fairly recently got together and were obsessed with one another, YLAF was just our 'time out', wasn't it? We had a lot of challenges, and it was four days of absolute heaven in the year, at a time when we'd have to come home and deal with the unpleasantness of my family, basically. I suppose that's why, for us, the story of the rings and the story of having that special time together, outside of all that other stuff, is so important. ■

Stocking up on books at the Libertas! stall

Overleaf: Jackie Kay (LC)

2004-06

Members of the planning group set up to reboot the festival (L to R): Helen Shacklady, Helen Sandler, Jen Challinor, Jane Traies, Claire Mooney, Lois Wells, Ann Kaloski, Pat Thynne

RESCUING THE FESTIVAL

The shop finally closed on 17 December 2003. Working from home, Jenny and Ann continued to run Libertas! as a mail-order business, through *Dykelife* and the website. But the last bricks-and-mortar women's bookshop in the UK had closed its doors, and the Libertas! Lesbian Arts Festival was no more.

Or so everyone thought.

Among the voices clamouring for the story to continue, the loudest came from an unexpected direction. Over the years, the City of York Council had become one of the festival's staunchest supporters. They had seen what a boost the annual autumn event gave to the tourist trade: at a time of year when visitor numbers might be expected to fall, the Lesbian Arts Festival brought thousands of new customers to the city's hotels, shops and restaurants. Or, as a council officer observed, 'We can see your audience all over town!'

If Libertas! could not run the festival any more, the council asked Jenny, was there anyone else who could?

The wider lesbian community was of the same mind. The weekend was now an established highlight of the sapphic calendar – surely it could not be allowed to die? Jenny knew that running the festival without the bookshop would be too much for one person to undertake alone, so she began to talk to people who might be willing to work together to keep it alive.

As a result of her efforts, a group of volunteers came together to discuss a possible future for the festival. I was one of them, and still have a strong impression of our early meetings. The first was held in York on Friday 16 January 2004, in a historic

Guildhall committee room provided by council officer Peter Boardman – a champion of the festival. The women who gathered that day had a wide range of experience in the arts, events, education or the public sector. Just like the Libertas! customer base, some lived in York, but the rest were from places far and near across the UK. The locals were Jen Challinor, Anne Rippon and Jenny Roberts herself. Claire Mooney travelled to the meeting from Manchester, Helen Sandler from London, Helen Shacklady and Pat Thynne from Cumbria, while I had driven the 150 or so miles from south Shropshire. (Cheri Gillings and Ann Kaloski would also join the group, but were not able to attend this first meeting.)

There was a lot for this not-yet-constituted group to do. Helen Sandler offered to chair the meeting and Claire to take the minutes. The next day, Helen wrote in her diary:

> Yesterday was the first meeting of the 'York Lesbian Arts Festival, supported by Libertas!' (Perhaps it should be the 'National Lesbian Arts Festival at York'? Too late for that now.) We actually covered the agenda, and set up an organisation, in five hours!

Helen's reservations about the name did not go away, she explained to me:

> I'm from Manchester myself – I grew up there before moving to London for university – and I was very keen on the festival remaining in the north of England. But by keeping York in the name (which was also going to be the name of the company) we were assuring ourselves and the council that we would stay put, and there were downsides to that. For a start, it sounded like a local festival rather than a national one. And a future move to a larger, more cosmopolitan city like Manchester or Liverpool might have offered a bigger choice of venues and brought in a

bigger audience and more women of colour. As soon as the name 'York Lesbian Arts Festival' was on the table, Claire Mooney pointed out that it would be abbreviated to YLAF, pronounced 'Why Laff?' Claire was a funny woman, and we did all laugh when she raised it. It was not a great name for a fun event – especially as the humourless dyke was a common stereotype at the time – but we had so much to do that day, we just agreed the name and powered on. I did live to regret it, because I could see the confusion on people's faces whenever I said 'YLAF' to anyone new for years to come!

But the decision was made, and the 'York Lesbian Arts Festival' it would remain. It quickly became clear that staging a festival that year was out of the question: there was simply too much to do. A call to Arts Council England reassured the group that missing a year wouldn't affect our ability to make a funding bid immediately. So planning began for the now-traditional autumn date, but in 2005.

Although Jenny was on hand with advice and support, and the overarching aim was to produce a festival like the ones that had preceded it, the new business model had to be very different from that operated by Libertas! Without the bookshop behind it, YLAF needed to become a not-for-profit company in its own right, and to start raising funds.

None of the members felt able to take on responsibility for financial management, so finding a treasurer was a priority, too. By the end of May, progress was being made on all fronts: City of York Council had released £1000 in start-up funds (and invited Jenny to apply for more); the Arts Council seemed positive; and Lois Wells had shown an interest in becoming treasurer.

The team were still getting to know each other. Face-to-face meetings were only possible roughly every two months, since half the committee lived so far from York. But when we did meet, we established a habit of gathering at Betty's, the iconic tea rooms on the corner of St Helen's Square, for a convivial breakfast before business began. Claire Mooney remembered that time with affection:

> I thought the committee was great. Just phenomenal! Those early times… people were absolutely lovely. Meeting up at Betty's before we'd go for the meeting… The steering group had the attitude, 'We're all doing this together.' That's what I loved about it. It was a community. We had each other's backs – we were there for each other.

After the third meeting, Helen Sandler reflected more equivocally in her diary:

> It's strange being on a committee with people you don't know well. It is a case of learning people's styles, abilities and follies. Some talk it up and don't deliver; some deliver with no fuss; some seem to do nothing much. But they are all contributing to meetings. The next meeting will be a weekend at JT's house in Shropshire. Hopefully we will have time to socialise and get to know each other better.

Which was exactly what happened. There was much fun and laughter that sunny June weekend, as well as solid progress on festival business. The group was learning how to work together: a finance sub-committee was formed to support Lois as treasurer, and Ann Kaloski gave everyone a demonstration of how to use a Yahoo Discussion group. (These were the days before smartphones or social media; many of the committee were still having to 'dial up' on their landline to get an internet connection.)

Finance was high on the agenda. By this stage, it had become clear that the Arts Council grant would be significantly smaller than hoped. The original plan had been to fund two paid posts

– a festival director and an administrator – but the committee now agreed that the administrative post would have to go, and we would continue to do most of that work ourselves on a voluntary basis, as well as looking for additional sponsorship. A job description for the post of festival director was drafted. The group spent an enjoyable afternoon brainstorming about how the festival might look, producing a long wishlist of favourite authors and performers. We agreed that an indoor marketplace for lesbian businesses would be a great addition to the festival and a possible money-spinner. Libertas! would retain exclusive rights to sell books.

At that point, the committee assumed Jenny and Ann would be running the stall. However, working from home packing and posting books, without any face-to-face interaction with

Seraphina Granelli (left) was to become manager of the new-style Libertas! business *(HS)*

Ann Kaloski and Pat Thynne at a mini festival organised by Jenny as a fundraiser in May 2005 *(HS)*

their customers, was proving tedious and later that summer, Jenny announced that she was selling the remaining Libertas! business to *Diva*. Helen noted in her diary: 'I didn't see that coming! The implications for YLAF are many and various.' Jenny suggested asking Kim Watson, marketing director at *Diva*'s parent company Millivres Prowler Group (MPG), for help to ensure the festival went ahead, in exchange for the rights to run the bookstall.

Meanwhile, the steering group's work continued, and in October 2004, YLAF was registered at Companies House. The directors were listed as Ann Kaloski (chair), Jane Traies (secretary), Lois Wells (treasurer), Jen Challinor, Claire Mooney, Anne Rippon, Jenny Roberts, Helen Sandler, Helen Shacklady and Pat Thynne. The Memorandum of Association set out the aims we had agreed: to stage an annual arts festival that would celebrate the diversity of the LGBTQ women's community; to

Helen Sandler (left) and Cheri Gillings at the mini fest (HS)

create a safe space that was welcoming, inclusive and accessible; and (in line with Jenny's original hope) to promote the wider acceptance of LGBTQ culture in and around the City of York.

The first action of the new company was to appoint Helen Sandler as festival director (part-time and freelance). She was ideally qualified, as an author, editor and reviewer who had been involved with the Libertas! events from early on. Helen told me:

> The cogs were whirring away in my brain before I ever asked the committee about the job. Having worked for both Diva Books and *Diva* magazine, I had ideas for how MPG and YLAF could work together and was itching to sit down with Kim and discuss them. Could they provide enough sponsorship money to pay for a festival director? If so, maybe I could take on that role? It all depended on what the committee thought, but I even wrote in my diary:

'Looming large in my mind are the possibilities for my own advancement. That is the most brutal way of putting it.' I don't have that sort of drive any more, but in my thirties I was always looking for the next big project, and admittedly that was partly about status, but also doing new things, the thrill of the new. I was delighted when I got the job, but nervous too.

Helen was reassured to know she would have Jenny's experience to lean on. Jenny's advice, set out in a document called 'General Organisational Notes', begins:

The festival has been a success because it worked – every year. This only happened because of *absolute paranoia* about the event going badly wrong. So, my main advice is: Be paranoid. This festival is just a small step away from being a disaster.

Jane Traies (right) and Jacky Bratton at the mini festival *(HS)*

Fortunately, the list also included lots of practical tips, such as:

> Do not let people into sold-out events without a ticket (even if they make a scene – and they will).
> Do not replace lost or stolen tickets. (Typical excuses are 'I can't remember where I put them' / 'My ex stole them.')

It was a relief for everyone that Jenny was still in the picture. Since there had been no arts festival in 2004, she staged a 'mini YLAF' of author readings at St John's College in May 2005. This served as a fundraiser and promotion for the main event and was an opportunity to sell advance tickets.

Even so, the board realised early on that they were not going to meet their ticket sales target, and revised it downwards, reducing some other costs to compensate. The total YLAF budget was around £120,000 and the new director's first priority had to be money. A quarter of income was expected to come from grants, with the Arts Council grant forming the bedrock – but even that, as Helen was to discover, was precarious:

> Their representative was always helpful. But every year, she said, 'I must remind you that we are not giving you *annual funding* for your festival. We're funding it each year *as a new event*, and each year you have to have new stuff in it to make it worthwhile for us to fund it.'
> And that was a struggle for us. Because really, we *were* putting on a similar festival every year, and they always wanted to see what was new. That was another reason for bringing in partnerships with small organisations like Club Wotever, and so on. Because then you could show you were doing something new each time.

In return for the involvement of the Libertas! and *Diva* brands, Kim Watson had agreed the company would support the festival to the value of £24,000 in cash and in kind. The new-style Libertas! would publicise the festival, act as ticket agent and run the bookstall. *Diva* magazine would also offer marketing and have a presence at the festival. This package made MPG the main sponsor.

In order to make the 2005 festival sustainable, Helen and the board worked hard at finding other sources of sponsorship, too. They developed partnerships with a wide range of smaller organisations, many of which gave in-kind sponsorship rather than money: for instance, mutual publicity deals or air fares for authors. Invisible to festival attendees except as a logo or an acknowledgment in the programme, such sponsorship was crucial, and obtaining it was a time-consuming job. In the end, as well as being funded by Arts Council England, YLAF was financially supported by more than a dozen sponsors and partners.

A frantic festival director noted in her diary on 20 October: 'One week to go. The things that might yet go wrong are the things I don't really understand: licences, permissions, insurance, accidentally breaking the law or the local custom.'

But there was no time to go on a crash course. Ready or not, on the last weekend in October 2005, after nearly two years of hard work, the festival made its triumphant return to York. ∎

libertas
York Lesbian Arts Festival
YLAF 2005

Souvenir Programme

£3 (proceeds towards next festival)
Exclusive mini Cameron McGill mystery

Friday + Saturday Book Festival

Two days of the best in lesbian writing with forty top authors and new voices

Authors + speakers

RV Bailey
RV Bailey, who was born and brought up in Whitley Bay, Northumberland, worked as a cafeteria assistant, librarian, information officer, teacher, counsellor and lecturer before retiring. The other voice in poetry recordings by her partner UA Fanthorpe (Awkward Subject, Double Act, Poetry Quartets 5 etc) is that of RV Bailey. They live in Gloucestershire. Her first full collection of poetry, Marking Time, was recently published by Peterloo.

Jay Bernard
Jay has been on the performance poetry scene for about two years. She was the winner of the London Respect Slam 2004 and has since become a 'slambassador'. This has led to performances at The Human Rights Watch in Shakespeare's Globe and the 7/7 vigil in Trafalgar Square, as well as a feature in the Guardian. Jay has performed on television and radio and been published in Poetry London.

Joanna Briscoe
Joanna's first novel, Mothers and Other Lovers, about a girl having an affair with her mother's best friend, won a Betty Trask Award. Her second, Skin, is about the beauty industry and the mutilation of women's bodies. It was runner-up for the Encore Award. Her latest novel, Sleep with Me, was a lead title for Bloomsbury in July. Joanna lives with her partner Charlotte Mendelson and their two children in north London and is working on a contemporary gothic novel.

Louise Carolin
The deputy editor of Diva, Louise has written for the magazine since 1994. Louise has contributed to Butch-Femme: Inside Lesbian Gender (ed. Sally Munt) and Acts of Passion, Sexuality, Gender & Performance (eds. Nina Rapi & Maya Chowdhry). She has also published poems and a short story. She is pursuing a part-time PhD at Sussex University on lesbian and gay magazine collectives in the 1980s, having worked for both Shocking Pink and Square Peg.

Maya Chowdhry
A poet, playwright and interactive artist, Maya has won the BBC Radio Young Playwrights Festival with Monsoon and the Cardiff International Poetry Competition with Brides of Dust. She was a member of the editorial collective of Feminist Arts News and co-edited Acts of Passion: Sexuality, Gender and Performance. Maya was writer-on-attachment at the National Theatre Studio in 2002 and is working on a collection of digital poetry, destinyNation, for which she received an Arts Council literature award.

Fiona Cooper
Fiona Cooper has published a collection of short stories and eight novels including Rotary Spokes, Jay Loves Lucy and most recently As You Desire Me (Red Hot Diva). She lives and works in the north-east of England, as a writer, medium and soul therapist. She is researching a book about the late performer Nancy Cole – whom she first saw at the York Arts Festival in 1973. She teaches creative writing, as well as performing her work on radio, across the country and in Europe.

Jane Czyzselska
As editor of DIVA, Jane Czyzselska has rebranded and increased circulation of the monthly glossy for lesbians and bisexual women. Jane was previously a regular contributor for The Times, Independent, Observer, Guardian, Gay Times, Attitude, Big Issue and Pink Paper. She has also worked as editor of the gay and lesbian lifestyle website Queercompany, as an online editor at the BBC and as contributing features editor of Fable magazine. She recently appeared on Richard and Judy.

Stella Duffy
Stella Duffy has written ten novels. Parallel Lies (Virago) and Mouths of Babes, the fifth in the Saz Martin series (Serpent's Tail) were both published this year. State of Happiness was longlisted for the 2004 Orange Prize and Stella is writing the screenplay. With Lauren Henderson she was co-editor of Tart Noir, from which her story Martha Grace won the CWA Short Story Award. She writes short stories and features as well as writing for radio and theatre. Stella is an actor, improviser and workshop leader.

UA Fanthorpe
UA Fanthorpe was born in 1929. She taught at Cheltenham Ladies' College but it was while working as a hospital receptionist that she started writing poetry. Her first volume, Side Effects, was published in 1978 by Peterloo Poets, followed by seven more, including Queueing for the Sun (2003). A new Collected Poems came out this year. UA has been awarded a CBE and the Queen's Gold Medal for Poetry and has appeared on Desert Island Discs. She lives in an Elizabethan cottage with her partner Rosie Bailey.

Jane Fletcher
Jane Fletcher is the Gaylactic Spectrum Award shortlisted author of two fantasy/romance series: The Celaeno Series and The Lyremouth Chronicles. The latter (The Exile and the Sorcerer, The Traitor and the Chalice, and The Empress and the Acolyte) are to be published by Bold Strokes Books in 2006. Born in Greenwich, London in 1956, she lives in south-west England where she keeps herself busy writing both computer software and fiction, although generally not at the same time.

Susan Hawthorne
Susan is publisher at Spinifex Press and research associate at Victoria University in Australia. Two of her books have been selected as among the year's best: The Falling Woman (novel, 1992) and Wild Politics (political theory, 2004). Her new poetry collection, The Butterfly Effect, is due out in 2005. She has edited or co-edited nine anthologies, including September 11 2001: Feminist Perspectives (2002); Cat Tales (2003); and HorseDreams (2004). Susan is also an aerial performer and has written many pieces for performance as a member of both the Women's Circus and the Performing Older Women's Circus.

Karin Kallmaker
Karin Kallmaker is descended from Lady Godiva, a fact that pleases her and seems to surprise no one. The author of more than twenty novels (including the award-winning Sugar and Maybe Next Time), she recently expanded her repertoire to include erotica with All the Wrong Places. As Karin says, "Nice Girls Do". She fell in love with her best friend at 16 and still shares her life with that same woman, and their two children, nearly 30 years later.

Ann Kaloski
Ann Kaloski is a lecturer at the University of York Centre for Women's Studies. One of the founders of Raw Nerve Books, a small feminist press, she co-edited White?Women: Critical perspectives on race and gender, and Celebrating Women's Friendship. Ann is the chair of the steering group that runs the York Lesbian Arts Festival.

Jackie Kay
Jackie Kay grew up in Scotland. Her poetry collections include The Adoption Papers, Other Lovers, Off Colour and, this year, Life Mask (all from Bloodaxe). Her fiction includes a novel, Trumpet (Picador, 1998) and a book of stories, Why Don't You Stop Talking (Picador, 2002). She has won many awards, is a Fellow of the Royal Society of Literature and teaches Creative Writing at Newcastle University. Jackie lives in Manchester with her son.

Renate Klein
Born in Switzerland, Renate has lived in Australia since 1986. Her books include anthologies on science and women's studies as well as authored books The Exploitation of a Desire and RU 486: Misconceptions, Myths and Morals which was highly commended in the Human Rights Awards. Renate is co-founder and publisher at Spinifex Press which has just brought out her new book Radical Reckonings: Women's Lives, Men's Technologies.

VG Lee
VG Lee is the author of two humorous novels, The Comedienne and The Woman in Beige, both published by Diva Books. She writes for Velvet magazine and gives readings all over the UK. She also teaches creative writing. Val moved from London to Hastings a couple of years ago and her experiences on the south coast have inspired The Diary of a Provincial Lesbian, out soon from Onlywomen Press.

Aoife Mannix
Aoife is an Irish writer whose first full collection of poetry, The Elephant in the Corner, was published in July by Tall Lighthouse. Her work has appeared in magazines and anthologies including Velocity (the best of Apples and Snakes) and been broadcast on BBC radio. In 2003 she recorded a spoken-word CD, Did You Forget to Take Your Tablets?, with musician Richard Lewis and she is featured on the Voices From The Lighthouse CD. Aoife performed as part of the 'Kin' spoken-word tour organised by Renaissance One.

Valerie Mason-John
Valerie Mason-John aka Queenie is the author/editor of Making Black Waves and Talking Black, which document the lives of African and Asian lesbians in Britain. Her plays Sin Dykes and Brown Girl in the Ring received critical acclaim. She has been named as one of Britain's Black Gay Icons, worked as artistic director of London Mardi Gras Arts Festival and launched a lesbian beauty contest. Valerie's novel, Borrowed Body, and a non-fiction book,

Detox Your Heart – ways of working with anger, hatred and fear – were both published recently.

Val McDermid
Award-winning crime writer Val McDermid grew up in Kirkcaldy on the East Coast of Scotland and now divides her time between Manchester and Northumberland. She writes for national newspapers and broadcasts on BBC Radio. Recent books include the Lindsay Gordon mystery Hostage to Murder; the Tony Hill/ Carol Jordan novel The Torment of Others; and a collection of short stories, Stranded.

Claire McNab
Claire McNab is the author of 50 books including the Carol Ashton, Denise Cleever and Kylie Kendall series of lesbian mysteries. Claire teaches novel-writing in the UCLA (University of California, Los Angeles) Extension Writing Program.

Raman Mundair
Currently Scottish Arts Council writer in residence at Glasgow Women's Library, Raman is a writer, artist and academic and an experienced workshop facilitator. Her poetry collection, Lovers, Liars, Conjurers and Thieves, is published by Peepal Tree.

Jacqueline Phillips
Jacqueline Phillips is the author of 121 Days of Sodom. She is thirty-two years old, holds a degree in psychology from Staffordshire University, and is currently teaching. Her second novel is with a publisher and she is working on ideas for a third.

Radclyffe
Radclyffe, having practised surgery for thirty years while writing for pleasure, established Bold Strokes Books, a US lesbian publishing company, in 2004, and later retired from medicine to write and publish full-time. Her lesbian romances include Safe Harbor and its sequels; plus two romance/intrigue series: the Honor series and the Justice series, of which Justice Served came out in June. As a follow-up to Change of Pace: Erotic Interludes, she recently co-edited Stolen Moments: Erotic Interludes 2 (September 2005) with Stacia Seaman. Her upcoming works include Honor Reclaimed (December) and Turn Back Time (February 2006).

Jenny Roberts
Jenny Roberts was born a boy but changed to her correct gender in 1996 at the London Bridge Hospital. She founded the Libertas Women's Bookshop in 1998, and the Libertas Lesbian Arts Festival which took place in York from 2001 to 2003. She continues to support the festival as a member of the steering group of the new company. Her first two Cameron McGill mysteries, Needle Point and Breaking Point, were published by Diva Books in 2000 and 2001 and are now reprinted by Three Corners Press. The third, Dead Reckoning, was published by Diva Books in May.

Helen Sandler
Helen is the author of a comedy of madness, The Touch Typist, and an erotic novel, Big Deal. As commissioning editor of Diva Books, she edited three collections of lesbian fiction – The Diva Book of Short Stories, Groundswell and Necrologue – two of which won Lambda Awards. She has performed

her poems at Book Slam and published them in Suspect Thoughts and the new issue of Chroma. Helen is the festival director of YLAF 2005 and edits the books pages of Diva magazine.

Shamim Sarif
Shamim's first novel, The World Unseen, received the Betty Trask Award. Her second, Despite the Falling Snow, is part love story, part thriller. Set between cold-war Moscow and present-day Boston, it tells of passion, betrayal and lost love. Her screenplays based on the books are being produced by Enlightenment Productions, which she runs with Hanan Kattan. Shamim is 35 and lives in London with her partner and their two children.

Manda Scott
Manda Scott is a writer, climber and would-be dressage rider. Her first novels were contemporary crime thrillers for which she was shortlisted for the Orange Prize and the US Edgar Awards. More recently, she has embarked on a series of four historical novels portraying the life of the woman we know as Boudica and the revolt she led against Roman occupation. Dreaming the Eagle, Dreaming the Bull and Dreaming the Hound are in print and the fourth is in progress.

Helen Shacklady
Helen has an MA in Arabic Studies and has had spells as a university lecturer, a canteen lady and a second-hand bookseller. She lives in Ulverston in Furness and is a housekeeper at Swarthmoor Hall (the cradle of Quakerism), where she counts sheets and makes soup. Helen is on the steering group of YLAF, and relaxes by trying to grow vegetables on an allotment. Her latest novel is The Vinland Sheep, a romance set in the Wars of the Roses.

Cherry Smyth
Cherry is the author of Damn Fine Art by New Lesbian Artists and Queer Notions. Her debut poetry collection, When the Lights Go Up, was followed this year by The Future of Something Delicate (Smith/Doorstop). She has worked as a writer in residence in a women's prison and for the Prudential. She is poetry editor of Chroma, a queer literary journal.

Diana Souhami
Diana Souhami is the author of stylish biographies about rich and famous lesbians: Gertrude Stein and Alice B Toklas, Violet Trefusis, Radclyffe Hall, the 1920s society painter Gluck, Romaine Brooks and Natalie Barney. Selkirk's Island won the Whitbread Biography Award. Her forthcoming book Coconut Chaos focuses on Pitcairn Island, the mutiny on the Bounty and chance liaisons with unsuitable lesbians.

Clare Sudbery
Clare has been a Scrabble fanatic, a trapeze artist, a lesbian, a bisexual, a maths and philosophy graduate, a cleaner, a revolutionary socialist, a raver, a novelist, a dodgy performance poet, a singer, a shop steward, a gibbering wreck, a vegetarian women-only workers' co-op member and a meat-eating heterosexual computer programmer. Her first novel The Dying of Delight was published by Diva Books in 2004. She lives in Manchester with a toddler and a journalist.

Louise Tondeur
Louise grew up in Dorset and studied drama at the University of East Anglia. She became a drama teacher before returning to UEA to do the MA in creative writing. She has written two novels: The Water's Edge, and The Haven Home for Delinquent Girls, both with Review. She was pleased to be given a box of cakes at the Mini Lesbian Arts Festival in May and always welcomes a good cream bun. Louise is a lecturer in creative writing at Roehampton University and lives in London.

Jane Traies (Jay Taverner)
Jane Traies is co-author of the 'Jay Taverner' novels: Rebellion, Hearts and Minds, and Something Wicked. Having retired from a career in teaching, she works as a consultant, serves as secretary of the YLAF steering group and lives in the Shropshire countryside where the novels are set.

Helen Walsh
Born in Warrington in 1977, Helen moved to Barcelona at the age of 16. Working as a fixer in the red light district, she saved enough money to put herself through language school. Burnt out and broke, she returned to England a year later and now works with socially excluded teenagers in North Liverpool. Her first novel, Brass, is published by Canongate.

Sarah Waters
Sarah's first novel, Tipping the Velvet, won a Betty Trask Award. For her second, Affinity, she was awarded the Somerset Maugham Prize and the Sunday Times Young Writer of the Year Award. Fingersmith was shortlisted for the Orange Prize and the Man Booker Prize and won the CWA Historical Dagger. She is one of Granta's Best of Young British Writers. Tipping the Velvet and Fingersmith have both been televised by the BBC. Sarah's next novel, The Night Watch, will be published in February.

Christine Webb
Christine Webb was born and brought up in Newark, Nottinghamshire. She has worked as a teacher in Kent, the West Midlands, Berkshire and inner and outer London, and now lives in Buckinghamshire with her partner of many years. Her short story Miss Manifold appeared in the 2002 Diva anthology Groundswell, and she is (still!) working on a lesbian historical novel. After Babel, published last year by Peterloo, is her first poetry collection.

And there's more: erotic novelists Crin Claxton and Robyn Vinten reading from Va Va Voom, Cathy Bolton and Janet Swan of the Big Gay Read, writers from Manchester's Commonword and from the latest issue of Chroma, members of the Muslim group Imaan, the reincarnations of Vita and Virginia… In fact, too many to list here. You will just have to sidle up to them if you want to hear their life stories.

Changes to programme: Sandi Toksvig and Louise Welsh are each unable to take part because of other commitments.

Author photographs: RV Bailey and UA Fanthorpe by Laurence Cendrowicz, Stella Duffy and Sarah Waters by Charlie Hopkinson, Susan Hawthorne by Naced, Renate Klein by Susan Hawthorne.

Have your books signed personally!

All the authors will be pleased to sign their books for you. Just make your way to the ground floor after each panel or reading, buy the authors' books from the Libertas stall and visit the signing area to have them signed for yourself or as a gift for a friend or lover.

Thursday night
DIVA Cabaret

A thoroughly queer evening of comedy, poetry + song, starring the much-loved Clare Summerskill and the cream of the sapphic circuit, brought to you by our very own Claire Mooney

Claire Mooney
Singer songwriter Claire Mooney is a seasoned professional. She possesses the rare ability to blend music with social comment and affairs of the heart. Her albums have received national critical acclaim with Ordinary Rebel playlisted on BBC Radio 2. In constant demand as a performer and workshop facilitator, she works all over the country at a variety of venues. Earlier this year, she performed on BBC Radio 4's Woman's Hour and enjoyed a lively debate with GMTV's Penny Smith. She is also Concert Director for this year's YLAF.

Clare Summerskill
Clare performs stage shows, stand-up and comedy songs to lesbian and gay audiences up and down the country. She brings dyke humour to the forefront of alternative comedy and was recently seen on the Richard and Judy Show on Channel 4. As a writer Clare contributed to the last series of Weekending on BBC Radio 4. She wrote the award-winning lesbian musical An Evening With Katie's Gang which was produced at the Oval House, London. She was awarded a grant by the Arts Council to write and produce a play based on the memories of older lesbians and gay men entitled Gateway to Heaven, which toured to theatres around Britain last spring. Clare has had two short stories published to date. Single Again is to be found in the Diva Book of Short Stories, and Maggie Maybe in Groundswell (both edited by Helen Sandler). Clare has produced three albums to date. Her latest CD, Feels Like Coming Home, consists of original songs written and performed by herself and her band. She is working on a new album which will be out in the near future.

Pauline Omoboye
Pauline Omoboye has been published in many anthologies produced by Crocus, Nailah, Arrival, Stride and Sista Talk, as well as in the local press. She has appeared on radio, television and in many theatres and schools throughout the northwest. She was voted the judges' winner of the Manchester Stage To Page Poetry competition in 2004.

Al Start
Al Start's music grows from a strong acoustic foundation. Her melodies are sweet, soulful and often hauntingly catchy. Her strong guitar accompaniment provides the perfect balance; but don't be lulled into a false sense of security... it may take a minute till you realise just what she is singing about! Quirky songs about cross-dressing neighbours, rentboys and missing cats are intermingled with touching reminiscences of childhood, surreal dreams and candid confessions. The first album, Lammas (2000), released with Al's band, Toucan, on Lone Coyote Records, brought rave reviews and full houses all over the south. This was followed by a solo EP, Sea of Stars (2003). Sales rocketed whilst supporting Horse on her UK tour (2004) as did her fan base. Now her solo album, Go, is receiving rave reviews across the media. Among those who contributed to it are Sheryl Crow's keyboard player, Mike Rowe, and Mark Knopfler's guitarist, Luke Brighty. For tour dates see www.alstart.co.uk

Dyke Marilyn
Dyke Marilyn, the queer bastard child of Marilyn Monroe and Jimi Hendrix, sings 'Dildos are a grrlz best friend' and opens up her book of ego revelations. You too can spread her pages wide to reveal her black roots growing up in Harlesden, her childhood crush on a gay Jamaican guy who walked like a D-I-V-A, her Catholic guilt on having sex dreams about Barbra Streisand, and her escape to a life of fantasy in a closet named desire! Dyke Marilyn is the creation of Maria Mojo who uses comedy, impersonation and da blues to expose a clash of alter egos including Ms Ross 2 u (Queer Child), Dolly Trailer Trash (stripping 9-5) & Miss Piggy! Her original self-penned songs on geetar include Badass Woman and Ego Addict. Ms Mojo has a BA (Hons) in Philosophy and Applied Psychology. She is researching mythical, queer, bi-racial, and emotionally challenged identities while preparing for an MA in Gender Studies at UCL. "Some like it HOT when Dyke Marilyn's on Top. So come and play if yer hard enough!"

VENUE: York Racecourse, The Knavesmire, off Knavesmire Road
SHOW: 6pm Venue opens
Ground floor bar selling drinks and snacks
7.30pm Theatre doors open
8pm Your host Claire Mooney plays a set before introducing Pauline Omoboye, then Dyke Marilyn who takes us to the interval
Then Al Start and Clare Summerskill
10.30pm Show ends (Programme subject to change)

Friday night
Celebration Concert

An uplifting night of music introduced by your glamorous hostess Miss Amy Lamé, featuring the legendary Julie Felix, plus Sheboom, Lorraine Ayensu, The Jam Tarts + Deep C Divas

Amy Lamé
Amy's varied TV career began as a travel presenter on BBC2's Gaytime TV, trotting across the globe in a plus-size polka-dot bikini. She then went on to develop and present The Staying In Show on C4 and has appeared on dozens of other programmes. Radio credits range from Woman's Hour and Five Live to the BBC London breakfast show she co-presented with Danny Baker. Awards include a Sony and an Olivier. Amy hosts the cult performance club night, Duckie, every Saturday in south London and she's looking forward to keeping us all happy tonight.

Julie Felix
Julie's music resists all labels and boundaries. She continues her 40th year in the music industry with a new CD, I Walk With Beauty, her first live concert DVD filmed on the Isle of Wight, and a huge UK tour, the Rainbow Tour, which coincides with the release by Track Records of a compilation CD called The Rainbow Collection. She is 'eclectic' to say the least, performing her own original material as well as Dylan classics, traditional Mexican folk songs or native American Indian chants. It is always an inspiration when Julie Felix performs. With enthusiasm, passion and humour always present in her messages of hope, Julie believes that the power of music can have a positive effect on our often harsh world.

The Jam Tarts
Take 2 pints of classic soul, 2 tablespoons of rock 'n' roll and a pinch of jazz and whisk into a heady mixture of dance anthems. Pour into a pastry case made from 6 Yorkshire dykes, 2lb of raw vocal power and 1/2lb of sax and trumpet mixed with the funkiest rhythm section around. Place onto a hot dance floor, add a light dusting of disco and now you're really cookin'! (WARNING: May contain nuts.) Appearances this year have included the Trades Club in Hebden Bridge and the Women In Tune Festival in Wales. The Jam Tarts are: Saffron Waghorn (Vocals, flute); Becca Ryan (Keyboards, trumpet); Boris Stock (Tenor and baritone saxophones); Michelle Noirmot (Guitar, backing vocals); Sandy Talbert (Bass); Rhia Swankie (Drums, backing vocals).

Deep C Divas
The lesbian acappella group from Yorkshire are proud to be celebrating with thousands of lesbians at YLAF 2005. 'Since forming six years ago, we've appeared at several international festivals, bringing our mix of glamour, glitter and feminist principles to Parisian bandstands and the Sydney Opera House. We have seven members and our repertoire includes everything from traditional folk songs to Chaka Khan. Our CD In At The Deep End is available at the special Festival price of £5. For more information please contact: deepcdivas@ntlworld.com'

SheBoom
Returning to York after their rave performance at the Libertas Lesbian Arts Festival in 2003, the Glasgow women's drumming group are 35-strong tonight and will use their wide range of drums and percussion instruments to play an infectious mix of rhythms, blending Afro-Brazilian, Samba, African, Latin American, Celtic and European influences. They play regularly at events and rallies all over Europe.

Lorraine Ayensu
A guitarist who writes and performs her own songs, Lorraine (on left of pic) has recently achieved national recognition for her track The Truth Is, which has been selected for the new release Freeness CD. (Freeness aims to profile music being created outside the mainstream industry and is supported by the Observer and Karma Download.) Lorraine has three recorded works and is working on a new album. She is highly rated as a live performer. Tonight she is joined by her long-time collaborator Norma Daykin on alto sax and wind synthesiser.

VENUE: Central Hall, York Uni, Heslington, York
SHOW: 7.15pm Doors open
8pm SheBoom followed by Lorraine Ayensu + The Jam Tarts, introduced by Amy Lamé
9.10 (approx) 20-minute interval
9.30 Deep C Divas, Julie Felix
SheBoom drum us out around 10.40pm
NOTES: Sandi Toksvig is unable to take part because of other commitments.
Programme subject to change.

A SAPPHIC IDYLL

The board members sat down to dinner together on the evening before the 2005 festival in the Italian restaurant which now occupied the old Assembly Rooms. It seemed fitting that we were starting our first YLAF weekend in the same beautiful space where the Libertas! opening party had taken place seven years before. Between the marble columns, every table was crowded with excited women. After a summer in which we had taken fliers about YLAF to all the major Prides, we had sold close to 5000 tickets for the various events to around 2500 individuals, raising £58,000. Feedback later revealed that nearly half of these ticket holders had never been to the festival before. Our outreach had been effective: York was full of lesbians again, and expectation was high.

The weekend was built on the successful formula of previous years, with a packed three days of music, books, film and workshops, concluding with the outdoor concert. MPG's presence included a huge Libertas! bookstall, now run by Seraphina Granelli; while Louise Carolin was deputy editor at *Diva* magazine, so also went to the festival as part of her job. Louise recalls travelling up on a packed Friday night train from London with *Diva* editor Chance Czyzselska (then known as Jane) and Raj Rai from the marketing team.

Louise says:

When we arrived at the Travelodge, Chance and I found ourselves sharing a room (expected) and a bed (not expected). I can't imagine many companies expecting their staff to bunk together, but there you go – the wild west world of lesbian publishing.

Louise Carolin (left) with colleague Kim Watson *(LC)*

I remember being nervous because I was going to be reading an excerpt from a short story I'd had published in an anthology of erotica, and although the book was billed as writing by lesbian and bi women, my story was one of the few with an explicitly bisexual theme. At that time, it still felt like bi women were allowed into 'lesbian' spaces on sufferance and the tacit agreement that we wouldn't mention (whisper it) *men*. I had a lovely, conspiratorial dinner with Cherry Smyth, who tried to encourage me to read from the bit of the story that involved a withering penis, but by the next day I'd sobered up enough to feel it was a bad idea and stuck to the other bit, which was all hilariously bad sex with lesbians. It went down very well.

But on the Friday afternoon, a discussion on the state of lesbian health and healthcare made her feel even more embattled:

In further evidence of the not entirely welcoming response to bi women, I remember a discussion about sexual health during which someone said, quite sincerely, that bi women were responsible for bringing STDs into lesbian communities, as if chlamydia, clap et al. are somehow spontaneously generated by male bodies instead of being ancient, opportunistic bugs that belong to no gender. The worst thing was, I didn't really know how to counter that argument, and no one else did either, so I suppose the whole room left with the notion that men are disgusting pus-ridden beasts and bi women are vectors of disease into lesbian communities...

Looking through the 2005 programme, the rich diversity of the authors and performers is striking. Onstage at the book festival were writers of all ages and lengths of career; novelists in all genres and from countries as far apart as Australia and the United States. Poets ranged from teenage 'slambassador' Jay Bernard (who went on to win the Ted Hughes Award) and Glasgow-based Raman Mundair who had published her first

Poet Raman Mundair (LC)

Singer Julie Felix (LC)

collection, to national treasures UA Fanthorpe and her partner Rosie Bailey. And at the concert, artists ranged from high-kicking veteran folk singer Julie Felix to local band the Jam Tarts, and from Clare Summerskill to a very young Al Start. Al remembers how much she had wanted to get into the festival and how pleased she was to be booked: 'I thought I'd really made it!'

Authors, artists and audiences alike brought their own joys and sorrows to York. This was the year that Jackie Kay held her listeners spellbound with a heartfelt reading from *Life Mask*, her poetry collection about her recent breakup. Other personal stories were less publicly acknowledged. For instance, Diana Souhami gave an enjoyable talk about *Wild Girls*, her biography of Natalie Barney and Romaine Brooks. She called the talk 'A Sapphic Idyll', which was what she had originally wanted to call the book but, as she recalled in our conversation:

Comedian Clare Summerskill *(A-I)*

> My publishers said no-one would know what 'sapphic' meant. Then, when it was published in America, I tried again, but they said no-one would know what 'idyll' meant.

Diana's research, and the wit and professionalism of her delivery, were impressive. However, her own memory of the occasion is tainted:

> There was a kind of mirror between art and life! Because a lot of the relationships in that book are very complicated, and fraught, and I was in the middle of a fraught relationship when I was there. We were at the end of our relationship, that stage when you know it's all up, but you still see each other. So, I was rather tense about the whole occasion. And there was this… elision, between art and life, because this was so much what happened among the lesbians in my book (and I don't think it's entirely exceptional among lesbians generally). But that was what was going on.

Another 'elision of art and life' at this festival was Stella Duffy's memorable one-woman show, *Breaststrokes*. Billed as a 'funny and moving solo show about her experience of illness and other journeys', it made a lasting impression. Manda Scott describes it as 'profound and visceral and brilliant'. Jude S was in the audience and remembers:

> It was a mammoth performance. Just her and the chair. The whole auditorium was holding its breath. You could have heard a pin drop. I don't think I uttered a word for the rest of the evening. It had hit hard, with my mother lost to breast cancer.

That particular performance was important for Stella, too. She told me:

> Doing *Breaststrokes* there, for me, was a really big deal. I'd done it at Battersea Arts Centre, where I'd first developed the show. I started working on it three years after my first cancer, and I toured it a little bit, to a couple of breast cancer charities, but sharing that material with that audience...
> I don't know the stats, but at the time I was fairly young to have breast cancer. It's gotten younger since, but it is still talked about as if it only happens to straight women. And yet, statistically, as a percentage of our population – certainly at that time – more lesbians were getting breast cancer. (I suspect it's probably still true.) So, for me, there was a homecoming in doing *Breaststrokes* there. Not least because of the amount of people who it touched. It wasn't their story, it was very personal to me, but it also touched on a lot of things that mattered to them. So that made a difference.

After all the work and worry, the 2005 festival was a great success. As the outdoor festival came to a close, with SheBoom drumming to a cheerful audience in York city centre (this time in pouring rain), the committee gave a huge sigh of relief, not

Stella Duffy in *Breaststrokes* (LC)

just for ourselves, but because we felt we had come up to the standard Jenny had set.

Feedback was enthusiastic: many comments were about the inclusive and empowering atmosphere. One woman who had travelled all the way from the Outer Hebrides said that she and her friends were overwhelmed and delighted by the experience, as they had previously only known four lesbians – each other. It was clear that women enjoyed the arts festival, but were also there to enjoy mixing with other lesbians at a lesbian event. One said:

> The women at the festival were warm and friendly. Although I was there by myself, I never felt alone, as sometimes one can have that feeling of being alone in a crowded place. When having a drink or a bite to eat at the bookfest, I had many women strike up conversation with me, likewise at the two concert evenings.

Another attendee wrote on the feedback form, 'I've just come out, at the age of 32, and I felt I belonged for the first time in my life.'

Many commented on the festival being a safe space where they could be themselves, which they couldn't always do in their everyday lives because of homophobia or isolation. Although Section 28 had finally been repealed by a Labour government in 2003, women who had spent decades in the closet did not necessarily feel safe to come out. It is a testament to the empowering effect of YLAF that, in the following week, at least two participants came out as lesbian at work. One of the authors, who was also a university lecturer, was keen to talk to her students about the festival, and so told them she was a lesbian. One of the organisers went home from YLAF and was motivated to come out to her colleagues in a large public-sector organisation.

Meanwhile, in the world outside, 2005 was a memorable year for the whole LGBTQ community. On 15 December, just a few weeks after the festival, the long-awaited Civil Partnership Act (2004) came into effect. Lesbians and gay men all over the country flooded into their local registry offices and, for the first time in our history, entered into legally recognised partnerships with similar rights and responsibilities to those enjoyed by opposite-sex married couples. Two decades later, when 'equal' marriage is available to same-sex couples in the UK, it is easy to forget just how mind-blowingly revolutionary the coming of civil partnership felt. Among those taking early advantage of the new legislation were Jenny Roberts and Ann Croft, who registered their partnership on 27 February 2006 with a joyful gathering of family and friends at the Grange Hotel, York.

The YLAF board members who attended the ceremony stayed on in York for their Annual General Meeting on 1 March, and started to plan for their second festival. ∎

Jane Traies, Pat Thynne, Helen Shacklady, Jacky Bratton, Jen Challinor *(HS)*

Jenny and Ann's civil partnership *(JR)*

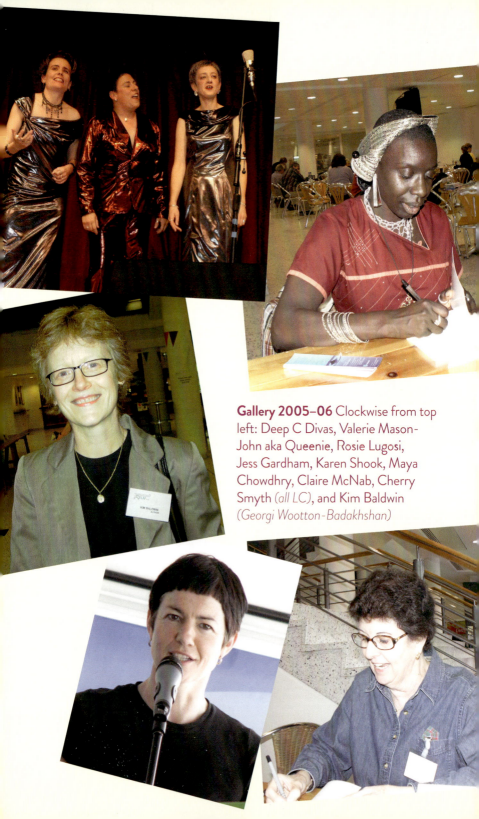

Gallery 2005–06 Clockwise from top left: Deep C Divas, Valerie Mason-John aka Queenie, Rosie Lugosi, Jess Gardham, Karen Shook, Maya Chowdhry, Claire McNab, Cherry Smyth *(all LC)*, and Kim Baldwin *(Georgi Wootton-Badakhshan)*

Val McDermid *(A-1)*

WRITERS + READERS

MANY OF THE MEMORIES I collected for this book came from people who had been quite overwhelmed by meeting their literary heroes in real life. Festival-goer Jude S was one:

> I remember being stuck in a lift with Val McDermid and an American crime writer, and Val asking me how it felt to be trapped in a lift with two murderous authors! I faintly gabbled some inane response and felt weak at the knees.

At St John's College, Dawn Jutton was equally overcome by Val's presence:

> I was smoking at the time, and me and Val McDermid stood outside having a fag, basically. And I was like, 'Oh my god, it's Val McDermid!' and then trying to act normal…

On one occasion a fan's excitement was misplaced, as Stella Duffy recalled:

> I was walking into the toilets, and this young woman followed me, and she went, 'Stella Duffy! Stella Duffy! I just want to say, you changed my life at secondary school! You made all the difference!'
> 'At secondary school? What was it that you…?'
> 'Oh your poems! They were so amazing, they made all the difference!'
> So I went, 'No, no, that's Carol Ann.'
> 'No, it was you!'
> And I went, 'Honest. It wasn't. It's very sweet of you, and yes, she's a dyke too – but it was Carol Ann. It wasn't me. Now can I go to the loo?'

Kate North (left) and Alex Southern *(A-I)*

Rebecca Brown (left) and Ali Smith *(LC)*

Went to the loo. Came out.

And she said, 'I'm sorry. I think it *was* Carol Ann.'

Hero worship wasn't confined to the audience, though. Kate North is a published author herself, and was a member of the YLAF board, but she was an equally bedazzled fan:

> I got to interview Ali Smith and the American writer Rebecca Brown for *Aesthetica* Magazine. I am a huge fan of both of their writing. I was very nervous, and completely blown away. I got to ask them lots about their writing practice and broader literary and cultural questions. But I also got to see them having a bit of a literary love-in, because they were fans of each other's work, also, and it was the first time they had met in person. It was a total fangirl moment!
>
> And I got Val McDermid to sign a book for my nan, who was a huge fan of crime fiction. I also sat next to her at a book signing. She had a queue a mile long and I had one woman and a dog. She was adorable to me.

The 'signing queues' were a feature of all the festivals and often crop up in people's memories. VG Lee remembers an experience at the Racecourse:

> I went down into the hall, and there was this huge queue at my table. I thought everybody had made a mistake! But no, they'd actually come to get my book signed, and that was so *smashing*! And people kept coming up to me and saying, 'We like your book.' It's such a lonely thing, being an author, and you get so few chances to read or meet your readers. It was fantastic! It really was so exciting.

Mia Farlane was just beginning to write at that time, and remembers how encouraging the more established authors were:

> YLAF was a series of star-struck moments for me, budding writer that I was. At the first YLAF, my partner Kristen

VG Lee signing books (LC)

Phillips and I got our copy of *Like* signed by Ali Smith. She added a smiley. I mentioned I was writing and she was just – 'that's great' – kindly encouraging.

At another YLAF, Kristen and I stayed, with friends, in rooms at an overheated building (you couldn't turn the heaters down) on the other side of a muddy York racetrack. Lots of chat and loud laughter in the communal breakfast room. I can't remember all the sessions I went to that year, but I do remember admiring the courage of the new writers.

I think it was at the last YLAF that I saw Sarah Waters – I spoke with her briefly, because I'd met her, by then, at a Morley College creative writing course. I told her I was making progress on my novel. The next day, Sarah asked if I'd be reading at the open mic event. She asked me this just before she was going up to read an unforgettable piece (involving a razor blade) from her then as-yet-unpublished novel *The Night Watch*. Such kindness.

It has been fascinating to hear the other side of this story, too: established writers talking about their relationship with the readers who came to the festival. Val McDermid, for instance, explained that for years she had had no feedback on her novels, either from reviewers or from her lesbian readers:

> Back in the early days, my books were never reviewed, because they were paperback originals, and newspapers and magazines just didn't review paperbacks, full stop. So when *Report for Murder* came out, it didn't get a single review. It sold, because people said to each other, 'You should read this book because I enjoyed it,' or 'because it's got lesbians in it.' So, to be in a room with people who had been there at the beginning was quite extraordinary – they'd come up with battered copies of the early Lindsay Gordon books and have them signed.
>
> York was the first time, really, that women came up to me and said, 'Reading your books made a difference in my life,' or, 'It was the first time I'd read a lesbian book,' or, 'It was the first time I'd seen a book with a lesbian protagonist, and it felt as if I had a place.' It was very moving for me to hear these stories. To hear that your books impacted someone's life – that's an incredible thing to hear, as a novelist. You write your book thinking it will go out in the world and hopefully people will enjoy it – but the idea that your books might change lives is quite moving, really. And people there had confidence to speak of their own lives in a way I wasn't exposed to before. So that's something I remember vividly about those early festivals.

Sarah Waters, too, experienced a different kind of relationship with her readers at the York festival. She told me:

Sarah Waters *(A-I)*

Val (left) and Betty at the 1940s-themed launch for Sarah's novel *The Night Watch* *(Alison Bechdel)*

As an author, one of the things I loved about the festival was that it seemed there was a lot of connecting going on between authors and readers. I got a lot of that when I was signing people's books, but also just wandering around, people would talk to me. I remember going to the café, all on my own, and getting a cup of tea and a Wagon Wheel. And someone from the audience came up and poked fun at me for eating a Wagon Wheel. And then later on, she sent me, through the post, via my agent, a Wagon Wheel! Also, as authors, we would do an event, but would also go to other people's events, be in the audience for them. And there was just complete permeability, it seemed to me, between authors and audiences.

Sitting in one of those audiences, in 2003, Lisa Hinkins remembers being fascinated by Sarah's revelations about her process as a historical novelist:

> She was talking about the fact that she'd been trying to get a light switch in a bathroom correct for the 1940s. And I was really impressed by the amount of detail she was trying to include.

In that same talk, Sarah wondered aloud if there was anyone in the audience who actually remembered the 1940s, and who might be interested in doing a historical review of the text. Betty Saunders and Val Bond, regular festival attendees from south Shropshire, volunteered enthusiastically. When the manuscript reached proof stage, Sarah sent it to them to read, and they had fun correcting little details such as the size and shape of 1940s petrol pumps, and whether cars had radios in the 1940s. When it was finally published in 2006, *The Night Watch* was shortlisted for both the Man Booker Prize and the Orange Prize. As a thank-you for their help, Sarah invited Val and Betty to the launch, a glamorous affair in the War Rooms under Whitehall.

L to R: Manda Scott, Jennifer Fulton, Val McDermid *(A-I)*

Another unexpected theme that emerged from the conversations I had with authors was the impact of spending time, not just with their readers, but with each other. As Manda Scott pointed out, although writers do meet at other festivals...

> This was different, because it was lesbian writers. That was completely unique. I don't do festivals any more, but in those days half of our lives seemed to be spent at them. The calendar was studded with 'Here's another writing event.' But YLAF was different. Usually, your publisher would say, 'You're going to Harrogate,' and you'd go, 'Oh, really? Am I? All right, then.' But YLAF wasn't a publisher thing. It was, 'We're going to YLAF because it's fun. We want to do it. No one cares about the brand!' So, it was a very different set of motives, I think. It was a chance for writers to get together.
>
> For me, there's something really special, when you're doing something as intensely isolating as writing a book, in getting together with a whole bunch of other people. You forget, then, that it is isolating; they are happy to talk about character and plot and semicolons and all the stuff that

Grainy evidence that Katherine V Forrest (left) met Jackie Kay (right) at the author dinner

nobody else in the outside world wants to talk about! So I remember the green rooms, and the conversations in the green rooms. I don't remember the details, but I remember that sense of 'This is necessary to the writing process, this capacity to sit with other people who *get it*.'

Val McDermid agreed:

As authors, we spend an awful lot of time sitting in a room staring at a screen or scribbling incredibly badly written notes to ourselves in notebooks, and we don't really get out to play much. So it's extraordinary, meeting people whose books you've read and enjoyed; being face-to-face with someone like Katherine V Forrest, for example, and being able to say, 'Your books made a difference to my life.' Because I know what it means to have that said to me.

And the lesbian writers I knew in the UK – we'd see each other occasionally, but we wouldn't get invited to festivals together very often. So it was good to be in a place where you could relax with each other and share experiences. It gave us a real sisterhood.

Sarah Waters recognised that sisterhood:

> You meet other writers at festivals, and I have writer friends I've met purely because I've seen them over the years at the same sorts of things – but for me YLAF was a really early exposure to encountering what felt like a community. We were there because we had this shared political and literary interest. So that did make it feel special. And the fact that you would go back year after year and it would be pretty much the same core of people.

Joanna Briscoe also appreciated the special quality of a women's literary festival:

> I went to YLAF twice, attending as a novelist in 2005 and as the partner of a novelist in 2002. It was something different and special: a very large gathering of gay women who loved literature. Right up my street!
>
> My now ex-wife and I had a child at the time of the first festival we attended, and it was an enjoyable and refreshing break to be away by ourselves in a hotel for the weekend, dancing, eating and hanging out with women. There was a warmth there, a sense of real fun, and so many authors to listen to.

Joanna found the festival less inclusive than some other authors did:

> In an unprecedentedly professionally successful year, when my bestselling novel was being televised and hers was Orange Prize shortlisted, we weren't invited as speakers, and later we were asked if we wanted to pay for tickets and come along as audience, which made us feel excluded but also amused. There was quite a dominant aesthetic at that time which we didn't really reflect, and this and the exclusion as speakers made us feel that at some level we were possibly not fitting into the club.

Joanna Briscoe *(LC)* Horse *(LC)*

Nonetheless, she remembers those she attended as 'highly enjoyable':

> They almost felt like a school trip for authors, with so many of us staying in the same hotel, listening to great work, chatting and dancing for hours. The size of it was exciting: this was a large and well organised festival that was important for lesbian literature, and it was great to be part of something like that at that time.

The sense of creative camaraderie was felt not only by the writers, but by performers too. Horse also spoke enthusiastically about the rapport between authors, artists and audience:

> It was one of the biggest things I've ever attended that was specifically *lesbian* – then and since. I think people tend to assume that my audience is always lesbian, but I'd say over the years it's been about sixty per cent straight. I suppose my most fervent supporters are usually lesbians, yes, but to see everybody, our community, all at once, in the same space, en masse, was quite mind-blowing.

I remember Val McDermid joined me onstage for a song. We sang 'Ship to Shore', one of my songs that she liked. Such fun! It was a real coming together, not just of audiences and performers, but of artists and creators who would never usually have an opportunity to gather together. So it wasn't just '3000 lesbians'. It was the creators coming together and meeting as well.

Val said to me once, 'How do you write a song?' And I said, 'How do you write a book?' They're different skills; but equally honed, practised over a long period of time.

Singing together was also one of Stella Duffy's memories:

Val McDermid's got a fantastic voice, Jackie Kay's got a fantastic voice. I wouldn't put my voice in their category. But I just remember being up in the hotel bar for hours, singing.

Jackie remembers it, too:

Before the singing began (LC)

I remember meeting Stella Duffy there, for the first time. Stella and Val knew each other, and we all hung out together. My mum was there, and Stella's from New Zealand and my mum and dad had met and married in New Zealand. So there's a big New Zealand connection. And we ended up having a massive sing-song: Val, Stella, my mum, and my partner Denise. It was one of those really great nights, where you felt you'd really gone through something together – into the wee small hours!

I met lots and lots of people – it was a bit overwhelming in some ways, but it did just feel very friendly.

Making everyone feel welcome at YLAF was important to the organisers. In our first year, board members had taken turns to staff the front desk and welcome people as they came in. The next year, that welcome stepped up a notch, as Hiraani Himona and Robyn Vinten created the Ministry of Unbridled Fun and Frivolity (MUFF). Hiraani had joined the YLAF board in 2006, replacing Lois Wells as treasurer. 'I said I'd only do it if it was fun,' she told me, airily understating her contribution. She had soon stepped up to act as interim chair of the board, and played an important supporting role in the later years of the festival. But fun was still the priority:

> I didn't actually get to see very much of the festival, because Robyn and I were on the front desk all the time, being lovely and charming to everybody.

Robyn had appeared at early festivals as the writer Ruby Vise, and later became an active member of the organising team. She and Hiraani had decided that while staffing the 'front of house' desk they would, in Robyn's words, 'inject a little bit of glamour into the proceedings'. The two friends led the MUFF team, who were on hand to help answer questions, signpost festival-goers to places and events, and generally brighten people's day.

Robyn Vinten (R) and Reina Lewis adding style to the cloakroom *(LC)*

Hiraani recalled:

> We spent a lot of time on our outfitting. We put on our glamorous frocks every day, and we had chocolates on the front desk.

Stella Duffy remembers their welcome with particular affection:

> I remember how lovely it was, because I often suffer, like lots of us, from feeling I don't belong. It's really common: young people call it social anxiety. So, walking to the Racecourse entrance from the hotel, getting more and more nervous as I approached – even though I was doing one, two, even three panels and one of Crin's shows, or whatever – and being met at the door by Hiraani and Robyn, with chocolates, and just feeling like I was *allowed* to be there…

And they wanted me to be there. Yes, I was an author, so I was expected there, but it was also just feeling like I was welcome among those people.

That did make a big difference to me, because that wasn't my experience in every one of the writers' circles I mixed in. Not that people were rude, or horrid, but there was less… reaching out. And of all the book festivals I've ever done – and goodness, there must be hundreds! – I don't think I've ever felt so warmly welcomed, or so encompassed. ∎

Hiraani Himona bringing the glamour along with the spreadsheets *(LC)*

We have a winner! Robyn Vinten and Ali Smith draw the raffle (LC)

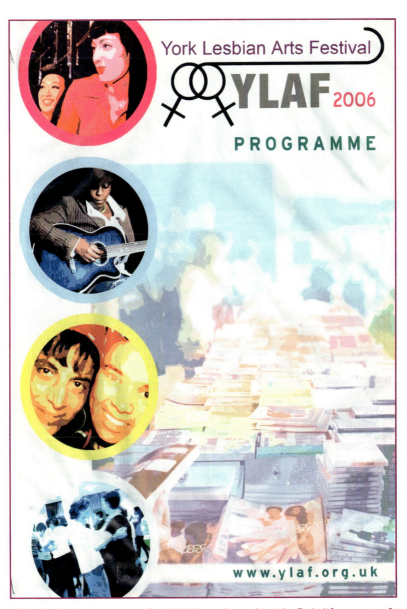

The festival programme for 2006 was bound inside *Dykelife* as part of MPG's sponsorship assistance

Poets Stacy Makishi, Salena 'Saliva' Godden, Aiofe Mannix and Dorothea Smartt with team member Jane Hoy *(LC)*

Latin dance workshop led by Studio LaDanza *(LC)*

A WEEKEND ON PLANET DYKE

FOR SOME FESTIVAL-GOERS who offered their memories to the making of this book, the Libertas!/YLAF years have merged into an indistinguishable tapestry of words and music; but every festival had its own special highlights, and 2006 was no exception. In her introduction to the printed programme, festival director Helen Sandler described it as a 'varied and vibrant line-up'; Val McDermid called it 'a weekend on Planet Dyke'. There were panels and activities for all tastes, from Latin dance to a poetry cafe.

In one memorable session, participants could try editing an issue of *Diva*. Louise Carolin and her colleague Chance were there again on behalf of the magazine ('although this time we stayed in a much swankier hotel and were blessed with a bed *each*') and introduced the group to some of the challenges an editor faces. Louise recalls:

> We taught participants the basic tenets of magazine editing, divided them into groups with a loose brief and a blank flatplan, and then threw them a series of real-life curveballs inspired by the competing demands of our actual readers: More older women! More younger women! More parenting! More weddings! More politics! Less politics! More sex! Less sex! More fashion! More sport! More pages! Fewer adverts! Amazingly, both teams turned in a final result that very much mirrored the issue at that time on sale in shops.

Another interactive experience was hosted by Fiona Cooper, and called 'Dinosaurs and Dykes'. Fiona's memory of that event is as colourful as the session itself:

Fiona Cooper centre stage for 'Dinosaurs and Dykes', ably assisted by audience members and friends including Jane Traies (left) *(LC)*

Picture this. Four hours' sleep and I'm driving my twenty-year-old Celica convertible somewhere beside the crazy river where willow trees make teepees in forty shades of green. I'm driving windblown and head to toe in camo purple. My partner Jean is shouting, 'Faster! Faster!' In the back are two of my favourite people, Joan Opyr and Alison Clarke, screaming round the bends all the way to York Racecourse.

It had started with the *Weekly World News* – my favourite trash paper, now sadly defunct. The *WWN* had front cover stories like 'Bat Boy Found 200 Metres Below Ground!' There was also an agony aunt called Dotty Primrose. And all with *real* photos, so it must be true. The headline story that had inspired me was 'DINOSAUR DYKES DIED OUT' and a picture of assorted dinosaurs wearing lipstick, carrying handbags and blowing kisses.

But we didn't die out, did we?

We'd spent half the night making rainbow bunting of every kind of dyke we could think of. We had a giant lilac fluffy dinosaur – our parthenogenetic mother – and her huge papier-mâché egg, ten yards of bunting and, of course, costumes. Jane Traies wore my one-and-only designer jacket and became one of those louche and lovely wealthy dykes of the 1900s – think Radclyffe Hall, think Capri and Natalie Barney. Joan Opyr was Calamity Jane, with bootstraps, a gun belt and a plaid shirt (her usual dress). Alison Clarke was our Wicked Witch of the West, complete with green face and lethal stilettos. I grabbed a few lovely people from the audience to represent a pirate, a rock goddess, a Nobel Prize winner and, of course Queen Victoria, whose edict 'Women don't' made us legal (if invisible). And of course, we humbly acknowledged the Dinosaur Who Dared to Be Different.

But most of all, this was a laughter-filled tribute to the rainbow of women who fought and demonstrated and will never stop loudly celebrating our love, our differences and our joy.

After that white-knuckle ride through lesbian history, the politics of the present were represented by a serious topical talk from Celia Kitzinger and Sue Wilkinson, describing their recent court case challenging the UK ban on same-sex

Sue Wilkinson (left) and Celia Kitzinger *(LC)*

marriage. Celia and Sue, both British university professors, had been legally married in Canada in 2003, but on their return to the UK, that marriage was not recognised under British law. When the Civil Partnership Act came into effect here, their union was automatically converted to a civil partnership. The couple rejected this injustice and took their case to the high court, demanding to be treated as married in the same way as an opposite-sex couple who had wed overseas; but the judge ruled against them. The YLAF audience supported the pair enthusiastically, but it would be another eight years before the Marriage (Same Sex Couples) Act came into force in the UK and their overseas marriage was recognised as legal.

The disco on the Saturday evening – now called Club Diva – was as popular as ever, though there was a tense moment when the CD deck failed, but the wonderful Cheri Gillings stepped up and entertained a thousand women by singing a Snow Patrol song, unaccompanied, until it was fixed. This was also the year that the club night spread on to two floors of the Racecourse, with music for a range of tastes.

On Floor 1, the evening started with 'gender-bending performance and fun toonz' courtesy of Club Wotever and their dressing-up box; followed by non-stop dance music from Beat Roots. Meanwhile, upstairs, Studio La Danza led a Latin and Ballroom session; then Chance Czyzselska and Sadie Lee were the DJs for the rest of the night. Chance remembers the evening vividly:

> DJing was my side hustle. Obviously being editor of *Diva* was the main thing – but I did the Candy Bar with a couple of friends, and I did other little lesbian venues in London. YLAF was the biggest crowd I'd ever DJ'd to. There were about a thousand women on the dance floor.
>
> I remember Belinda O'Hooley coming up to me, because I wasn't getting them dancing to begin with. And she was like, 'I think you need to play more of this, or that – I think

these girls need this and that...' And she helped me to use the right music. And then, after a while, with her input, there were loads of people on the dance floor. I seemed to be playing all the bangers, all the tunes that just totally got them going. And I've never been so appreciated as a DJ as I was at YLAF. It was absolutely wonderful! People were coming up to the DJ booth and just going, 'Oh my God! Amazing! All the best tunes!' And I was a bit embarrassed, actually, because it was a bit over the top.

The Barbican Theatre was still closed for repairs, and the hall at York University which had housed the concert in 2005 had presented access problems; so, in 2006, the Celebration Concert (sponsored by Unison) was held at the Racecourse itself. The ground floor space held an audience of 700, tightly packed, and the more intimate atmosphere seemed to produce a special rapport between performers and audience. Lorna Brooks and Jennifer John sang beautifully together as The United Colours of Brooks and John. Sue Perkins – already well known through

Jennifer John (left) and Lorna Brooks (LC)

Sue Perkins (right) keeping Security happy *(LC)*

her TV appearances with Mel Giedroyc, but only recently embarked on her solo career – blossomed in front of an all-lesbian audience and was an instant favourite. A lot of women had entered civil partnerships since the previous festival, and a topical moment in Sue's act was when she 'married' two women she had matched up from the audience.

Claire Mooney, who organised the concert (and saw performers at both their best and worst) declared Sue 'absolutely gorgeous to work with'. Helen Shacklady agreed:

> Of all the top writers and performers at the different festivals, for me, Sue Perkins stood out as one of the most un-diva-like. Chatty, genuinely interested in others and appreciative of their efforts, she took time late at night after a bravura performance to compare pet photos with one of the lovely security women and hand out toffees. If it hadn't gone a bit sticky, I would have kept the one she gave me (and probably framed it).

In the same concert, Horse shared feelings of heartbreak with her many fans, in an emotionally raw performance still vividly remembered by many. Jude S told me:

> I remember Horse McDonald being very angry onstage. (I'm a big fan.) She was going through the aftermath of a difficult breakup. I had an uncomfortable sense that we were witnessing terrible distress in a public arena. I couldn't watch.

Horse remembers it, too:

> I was going through a difficult time personally at this point. I began to sing a song that encapsulated that pain and I just physically couldn't sing any more.
>
> You could have heard a pin drop. There was utter silence, because people knew I was struggling. The tears rolled down my face.
>
> Then Tracy, who was doing my backing vocals, said, 'Do you want me to sing it?' and I said, 'Yes.' And we hobbled our way through it.

But for Horse there was also a positive side to this distressing experience:

> Afterwards, I met the audience and they were incredibly supportive. There were people who were or had been in similar situations to me. They hadn't spoken about this before, so being able to say 'That happened to me too' and 'I understand you' was quite something – because these are not things people talk about or have the opportunity to exorcise. So it was an incredibly personal performance for me and for the audience; and the festival gave me that opportunity to be myself.

The women who went to York to see their favourite authors and performers might be surprised to know how much this kind of emotional support meant to their idols. Jackie Kay has a strong memory of a similar experience:

I read a whole story for the very first time that I'd never read anywhere else. It was called 'You Go When You Can No Longer Stay'. I was quite nervous about reading that story. But I just read it, and that was it. And at the end of that story, everyone in the room stood up. They stood, and they clapped for the longest time. And it was really incredibly moving. It felt like the whole room kind of supported me and knew that I'd gone through something difficult, and people had gone through their own things, and it was very... It wasn't so much that they were the audience and I was the performer, it felt more symbiotic than that. It was like 'call and response' in the blues.

That was the opening short story from *Wish I Was Here*. The collection was chosen for a special one-off Book Club session at the festival, led by Jane Hoy, who recorded at the time:

Once discussion started and women came out with their favourite story, there was no stopping them. We spent some time discussing the story about the woman who gave birth to a fox, and when Jackie arrived we asked her about it. To our amazement she said it was based on a dream she had before the birth of her own child.

Jane also assisted at another of the workshops on offer in 2006, 'A Song in Seconds', in which a group led by Claire Mooney was set the task of writing and rehearsing a festival song, to be performed at the outdoor concert next day. Calling themselves the 'Laffettes' and taking their inspiration from the number of tickets sold that year, they produced the unforgettable YLAF anthem '3000 Lesbians Can't Be Wrong' and performed it to the delighted crowd, who joined in the chorus with gusto. It was another unforgettable moment of lesbian visibility in central York; and one which, many years later, inspired the title of this book. ■

The Laffettes ready for action...

... and performing '3000 Lesbians' onstage *(LC)*

Family Feelings

Maureen, Helen, Rosie and Phil *(LC)*

Such was the family atmosphere at YLAF that both Helen Sandler and Jackie Kay invited members of their own families to the 2006 festival. Helen's parents, Maureen and Phil Sandler, attended in both the years when she was director; her sister Rosie visited too.

Maureen recalls that everyone was very welcoming: 'People knew we were Helen's parents and said how much they appreciated the fact that both of us had come along.' For some, this was a stark contrast with their own situation: 'I remember talking to somebody who said she couldn't tell her parents she was a lesbian. It wasn't something she could broach with her family.'

The authors and speakers were approachable and Maureen and Phil chatted with many of them too. 'There was a reception for festival supporters where Sue Perkins had the role of welcoming the guests,' says Maureen. 'I didn't know who she was at that point but she came over to talk to us and was so warm and friendly. We met all these writers who have gone on to be very big names – people like Jackie Kay, Ali Smith, Sarah Waters – and none of them was at all aloof or big-headed. Naomi Alderman was there with her first novel, *Disobedience*, about two women in an Orthodox Jewish community. I'd heard it serialised on the radio and said to Helen, "You should book her!"'

The 2006 book festival culminated in Jackie Kay's solo reading to a packed house. Maureen recalls: 'I've been to a lot

FESTIVAL STORY

of readings but never anything with so many women – just women – and there was such a lovely atmosphere. Jackie's performance was spellbinding. She had everyone in the palm of her hand, which is certainly not easy with a crowd of that size.'

Jackie Kay's mother – another Helen – was part of that crowd. It was her birthday and Maureen and Phil had been dispatched earlier to buy chocolates ('which was harder than you might think in a city known for its chocolate, because we didn't actually know our way around').

Everything was in place for a big surprise and when Jane Hoy presented Helen Kay with a cake, candles blazing, the entire audience launched into 'Happy Birthday'.

It is a story Jackie still loves to tell: 'It was really fantastic! I remember when my mum got back to Glasgow, she said to her neighbour, who'd lived across the road for fifty years (and who was slightly homophobic but we kind of loved her)... She said, "Isabel, *one and a half thousand lesbians* sang me 'Happy Birthday'. Top that, Isabel!"'

She adds: 'I still bump into people who went to YLAF. At different events, former "YLAFees" will come up to me and say, "I was there when it was your mum's birthday."'

Apart from the sheer joy of such moments, they were important at a deeper level, fraught with the message that our biological families *could* love us; and that, meanwhile, our family of choice always would. When I interviewed Horse about her memories of YLAF, she said, 'There was something about it, wasn't there? It was like being asked to a family event.' ∎

Helen Kay's birthday cake *(LC)*

Above: BSL interpreter Ffranses Wharton *(A-I)*
Below: Maureen Elliott on the access desk *(LC)*

MAKING IT WORK FOR EVERYONE

WHEN I THINK ABOUT the festivals at York, my memories are often of things that most festival-goers didn't see. Hiraani Himona reminded me of one such task behind the scenes:

> We relabelled all the toilets at the Racecourse as either 'Sanitary bins' or 'Not sanitary bins'. And I remember that to this day, because when I'm being lectured by young people about gender-neutral toilets, I say, 'We were doing gender-neutral toilets before you were *born*, darling!'

In the early days, I had appeared at the festivals as a writer, and hugely enjoyed reading to those enthusiastic audiences. I also loved moderating panels of other authors, which I did many times after that first baptism of fire at St John's. Mostly, though, I shared in this work behind the scenes. I drove across the country to York to committee meetings; contacted dozens of B&Bs to see if they would like to be on our list of LGBT-friendly accommodation; walked for miles on the streets of York with Helen Sandler, talking to the proprietors of bars, restaurants and coffee shops about whether they welcomed lesbian customers; signed people up to our Friends scheme; booked hotel rooms for authors and artists; liaised with dozens of stallholders for the marketplace; and spent an exhausting Bank Holiday Monday at Manchester Pride with Pat Thynne, standing in the sun, handing out YLAF flyers.

The hours of the weekend itself were long. Robyn Vinten reminisced about:

> Getting up at the crack of dawn to set things up; being the first people there and the last people to leave. Herding

everyone into taxis and buses at the end of the day. And then doing it all again the next day!

I remember those early mornings, too. I think I was the only natural early riser on the team – for most of them, a nine o'clock start required a big effort of will – so when the festival was on, I was usually the first person at the Racecourse, walking the quiet rooms, checking the desk, making sure everything was in the right place before the day began. I loved every minute of it.

Within the YLAF organisation, individuals came and went over time – by 2006, Maureen Elliott had taken over the role of treasurer from Hiraani Himona, who had become acting chair, and Kate North was company secretary – but the structure remained much the same: one paid post, the festival director, with overall responsibility for the whole show, and a huge army of volunteers. Anne Rippon organised stewarding and security teams; Elspeth Mallowan led the timekeepers; Helen Shacklady now oversaw the arrangements for those with access needs; Lenna Cumberbatch was the official

Lenna Cumberbatch (LC)

Crin Claxton (A-I)

photographer, as well as working backstage.

The work behind the scenes didn't stop when the festival began; and much of it involved diplomacy. When Crin Claxton took over as festival director in 2007, she saw it as part of her job to pour oil on troubled waters:

> I learned a lot about diplomacy working as festival director! I always tried to keep people on side. So if somebody, perhaps, had a great contribution to make, but they were a bit abrasive, or brutally honest about things, I always tried to take that in my stride, or tried to mediate when there were personality clashes.

As musical director, Claire Mooney knew the challenges well:

> Like, trying to get a building to fit enough lesbians in! Because for several years the Barbican was out of action,

Amy Lamé *(LC)*

being done up, and that was a really good venue. And you couldn't put everyone on. One act said they wanted to be on, and I said, fantastic, I'll put you in the outdoor concert; and they said no, they wanted to be on at the main concert; and I said, well, it's booked... Every event was the same to me, all just part of the whole, and I thought, why can't you just be part of it? It was really difficult. I look back, and I feel sad that I couldn't put half the people on. There were so many. And you were always looking for a bit of diversity. Also, you book people in the hope that they'll be as good as when you saw them, and sometimes they're not!

In that case, Claire added, the audience would make sure she knew about it:

We were massive, weren't we, at getting feedback? And bloody hell, didn't people feed back! You had to have a bit of a thick skin there. But there were stalwarts. Julie Felix, for example – a complete star. She was great. Longevity, and all that stuff. Some of the best artists were: Sue Perkins –

Salena 'Saliva' Godden *(LC)*

absolutely gorgeous to work with; Amy Lamé – completely delightful to work with; Clare Summerskill – a stalwart of the festival!

As Claire mentioned, representation and inclusion were very much on the minds of the programmers. Helen Sandler recalled some of the challenges and delights of programming the book festival:

> There were so many possible criteria for inviting someone to appear at the book festival. Firstly they were supposed to be part of the LGBTQ+ world but that wasn't always easy to ascertain. I became adept at asking cheeky questions of strangers, at a time when not everyone was out. Going up to Salena Godden, or Salena Saliva as she was then, after she'd done an explosive spoken-word set at a straight festival – maybe Port Eliot – and saying: 'I loved your performance and if by any chance you identify as lesbian or bi then perhaps you'd be interested in appearing at our festival?' That kind of thing.

I lived in London so I would be going to book launches and poetry readings there; but as I said, I was from Manchester originally and with the festival being in York, there was that connection to the north of England too. Anyone with a new book was an obvious choice, and it helped that I was being sent new titles with lesbian content all the time in my *Diva* role. But I also tapped into writing groups, queer magazines and anthologies, to find writers who weren't yet known to our audience. I was always on the lookout for new voices, younger writers and people of colour. That didn't mean the audience would diversify overnight, of course: it was older, whiter and more middle-class for the book festival than on the London scene or even at the YLAF club night.

I have a lifelong habit of over-programming events, and I did do that at YLAF, because I wanted to have everyone I wanted to have! Of course as the director, I didn't see much of it myself unless I was onstage. There's a lot of greeting and troubleshooting. 'Where's Sandi Toksvig? What do you mean, she's stuck on a train?' That kind of thing. I have zero memories of sitting in the audience, but I do remember racing from room to room, then getting overwhelmed and retreating to the back staircase for a quiet sit-down!

A major challenge – and a priority – for YLAF's organisers was providing good access for festival-goers with disabilities. Volunteer Nic Herriot, who was part of the access crew for several years, told me how it all began:

> Down in Lampeter, we have the Women in Tune Festival. First we went to it as paying punters, the next year as volunteers, and the next year I went as disability crew. 2004 was the international year of the disabled, and I worked with some seriously disabled people. I remember one woman in particular – which brings me back to YLAF, because afterwards, she came to that too. I'd worked with many

people with disabilities, but none as severe as hers: she had to be on a flatbed – she couldn't sit up. I remember writing down her words for her, in a writing workshop, and then she read it out. I got to know her and her girlfriend and their little toddler, who is now a young woman. So I learned a lot there – she taught me a lot. And I worked with other people with different disabilities, including the deaf and the signers.

And I thought, we need this at YLAF. So I emailed and said, there's a team of us, four women, we've worked at WiT, here's our skills, here's what we can put in place. All I'm asking for is access to the concerts and our accommodation. So in 2005, the four of us came in, and we put together this disability package. And when my friend from WiT got her tickets, she asked, 'Will you be doing the disability access?' and I was able to say yes.

Helen Shacklady was the board member with overall responsibility for disabled access. She remembers the difficulties all too vividly:

Helen Shacklady and Pat Thynne on duty (LC)

To be honest, from 2005 until 2008 my focus was less on the 'lesbianness' of the festival and more on the all-too universal barriers, even in modern buildings, to access for everyone. The role would have been impossible without the support of the outstanding, dedicated and calm volunteers. What a relief to be met with, 'No worries!' when I came up with a last-minute demand or a fiendishly complex seating plan. Yet, in spite of the volunteers' best efforts, I know we fell short for some women, for which I'm still sorry.

The Racecourse had pretty good physical access, but wasn't ideal for anyone with a hearing impairment, because it couldn't support an induction loop system. The system they used required people to sit within range of a device at the front of the room and of course others, including people with visual impairments, needed to go near the front as well. If anyone reading this is someone who rocked up early to grab a front seat for their favourite author or performer and was then moved back by me, I'm sure you'll understand. (And I won't dwell on reports that on Saturday nights some couples may have used the – admittedly spacious – disabled loos for purposes other than that for which they were intended.)

Finding available venues for the amazing concerts was a very different kettle of fish, and even my jaw dropped on occasion. In one august hall, we were assured that 'of course' wheelchair users could be accommodated. True, but only in a long, narrow, empty space right at the very back of the balcony where even someone with 20/20 vision would have benefited from a pair of opera glasses. That women who used wheelchairs might perhaps like to sit with their friends in the stalls, or might also have hearing or visual impairments, were clearly alien concepts. And was it in the same venue that there was no plan for evacuating people in wheelchairs if there was a fire? Or was that at the much more modern hall, where the auditorium could only be accessed by stairs, so that

JM Redmann's panel applauding the BSL interpretation *(LC)*

anyone with limited mobility had to use a small service lift? What were the architects thinking?

By and large, though, the efforts of Helen, Nic and the other access volunteers were remarkably successful. Many women with both visible and invisible disabilities were able to enjoy the festival, whether as audience members, performers or stallholders.

The wonderful British Sign Language interpreters were part of this accessibility drive, and rapidly became a popular feature of the festivals in their own right, often drawing their own applause at the end of an author panel. In 2006, for example, sisters Ffranses and Elizabeth Wharton were the signers at a particularly memorable session, in which JM Redmann chaired a discussion with authors Therese Szymanski, Radclyffe, Megan Carter (aka Frankie Jones) and Kim Baldwin, on the subject of erotic writing. As the readings became more and more explicit, the Wharton sisters never faltered in their interpretation of whatever sexual practice was being described:

on more than one occasion their spirited performance received an enthusiastic ovation all of its own.

Sarah Waters remembers the signers well:

> They were wonderful, weren't they? I don't remember that happening at other festivals. It's kind of routine, now, to have a signer, but it wasn't then. I remember doing a panel where we'd been asked to read from books that had been inspirational for us. And because of *Tipping the Velvet*, and *Fingersmith*, I suppose, I wanted to read a bit of Walter's *My Secret Life*. There are quite a lot of lesbian bits in *My Secret Life*, so I read a lesbian bit, and there was the poor signer onstage next to me, who had to sign all this saucy Victorian language. That went down quite well with the audience, as you can imagine.

Somewhat uncharacteristically, Val McDermid found herself in a similar situation:

> One of the things about YLAF was that you often ended up on panels that were not what you normally did. So, I kill people for a living, and although I've murdered dozens of people, nobody thinks that's what I actually do. But you write just one sex scene, and *everybody* thinks that's what you do in bed. It's quite bizarre.
>
> Anyway, this panel was about erotic writing, and I have a short story that has a fairly raunchy opening. And of course we had signers – they were terrific. By the end of that paragraph, *no one* was listening to me; they were all focused on the signers.

As Helen Shacklady said, achieving full accessibility was sometimes impossible. Nonetheless, YLAF was probably ahead of its time in what it achieved. As US author Joan Opyr remarked, 'I have never attended a festival or conference that was as well organised or as disability-access friendly.' ■

The team working on the 2006 festival in the hotel lounge, with (in hat) admin assistant Lou Gerring *(LC)*

Overleaf: Stella Duffy and Semsem Kuherhi in 'True Pride and Prejudice' *(A-I)*

2007
+ after

FIGHTING TO SURVIVE

AFTER TWO EXHAUSTING YEARS, Helen Sandler stepped back from the role of festival director. Crin Claxton, who took over in 2007, had been attending the festival as an author since 2002 and was passionate about keeping it going:

> I always appreciated how much care Jenny, and then Helen and everyone who was involved, had put in to the organising. Things like the authors' green room, the authors' hospitality, paying for the authors' travel and accommodation costs… Seeing to all of that was done with so much care: I felt so looked after. And then, the events in the Barbican were incredible. Like, these lesbians taking over the Barbican Centre, York! It was mind-blowing. You just felt so good, like we'd really made it, we were really there. We were visible lesbians. I fell in love – totally fell in love – with the festival.

YLAF had always been run on a shoestring, often only just covering its costs. Staffing was minimal. As Crin pointed out:

> I think a lot of people didn't know that there was only one person working all year round who was actually salaried and whose hours were there. And I worked far in excess of the hours I was paid to work! The programmers who organised concerts, films, the cabaret night and so on got paid a fee; but all the rest, the team leaders and so on, were volunteers.

So, when it became clear that planning for YLAF 2007 was taking place against the background of an accelerating cost-of-living crisis, there was little room to economise. Thanks

Crin Claxton introducing the weekend programme *(A-I)*

to careful planning and monitoring, the 2006 festival had come in slightly under budget, making a modest surplus of around £4,000 and, for the first time, the board had been able to establish a small reserve towards the future stability of the festival. No one could have foreseen how woefully insufficient that reserve would prove to be. As festival-goers, like everyone else, faced tighter restrictions on their spending, it was soon evident that ticket sales would not meet predicted levels. Reluctantly, the board decided that, for YLAF 2007 to be financially viable, it would have to be reduced to two days. Consequently, recalls Crin:

> It was sold to me as a part-time job! Can you imagine? I think the board felt, because they did a reduced festival in 2007, that it would be less work, and it could be a part-time position.

Keeping YLAF afloat in such testing times was a formidable

Julie McNamara in 'I'm Your Man' *(A-I)*

challenge. Nonetheless, backed by a hard-working board of trustees and a now very experienced team of volunteers, Crin produced a fabulous two-day festival. As well as the familiar author panels, book launches and writing workshops, there were innovative additions (billed as 'Fun and Funky Fresh events') that included Julie McNamara's comic monologue 'I'm Your Man', an idiosyncratic performance piece by Fiona Cooper called 'Fantastic Voyage', and the first appearance of the festival's very own am-dram group, the YLAF Playas, in a Jane Austen spoof, 'True Pride and Prejudice', penned by Crin. Stella Duffy was among the cast for that. She told me:

> I loved doing Crin's plays. They were such fun. Any chance to dress up! Never learned the fucking lines, though. None of us ever learned the lines – there wasn't time!

In another Funky Fresh event, the short film *Fem* by Campbell X opened a debate that addressed the question, 'What does lesbian

Book Festival Programme
Saturday 27th October York Racecourse

Time/Place	Event
9.30am Voltigeur	Welcome to YLAF 2007
9.45 Voltigeur	**Breakfast with...** Helen Sandler wakes up & smells the coffee with Val McDermid, Manda Scott & Charlotte Mendelson
9.45 Knavesmire	**Writing for Performance:** Stella Duffy talks about writing for theatre, film and radio with play and *[obscured]*

2007 BOOK FESTIVAL

[obscured] also on 2 floor.

11.00 Voltigeur	**Sexy Gay Read:** Crin Claxton gets hot under the collar with Jackie Kay, Jennifer Fulton and Fiona Cooper.
11.00 Knavesmire	**What a character:** Jane Fletcher, Ellen Dean and Marianne K Martin talk to VG Lee about writing characters & characters they love.
12.00	**Break:** Authors will sign books on 2nd floor
12.15 Knavesmire	**Open Mic Slot:** your chance to share your work. Perform your 5 min piece of prose, poem or song. Performance artist Julie McNamara comperes. Sign up from 9.30am at Info Desk or 12.00 at session.
12.45-1pm Voltigeur	**Fun & Funky Fresh Event:** Fantastic Voyage Short performance piece from Fiona Cooper Ever wanted to be filthy rich and irresistible to women? Do you long to drive a jeep or sing the blues? Whatever your dreams, come and see Fiona Cooper - she walks! (unsteadily) she talks! (incessantly) she fuels your every flight of fantasy!
1.15-1.30 Voltigeur	**Fun & Funky Fresh Event**: True Pride & Prejudice The real natures of Elizabeth Bennet and Mr Darcy Short performance piece from the YLAF PLAYAS: Why is Elizabeth so strangely attracted to a man? What will her terribly close friend Miss Bonnet think of him? And just what is Mr Darcy's secret? Stella Duffy, Semsem Kuherhi, Crin Claxton & Helen

Time/Place	Event
1.45 Voltigeur	**My Big Gay Writing Day:** Top writing tips. Authors describe their writing day and what they wear. Jane Traies talks to Val McDermid, Tricia Walker, VG Lee & Sarah Waters.
1.45 Knavesmire	**The Plot Thickens**...Helen Shacklady talks about plot with Charlotte Mendelson, Jane Fletcher, Manda Scott & Marianne K Martin.
2.45	**Break:** Authors will sign books on 2nd floor
3.15 Voltigeur	**Rhona Cameron in conversation with Helen Sandler** Comedian, Get-me-out-of-here Celebrity and writer Rhona Cameron talking about her debut novel The Easy Drinking Club.
3.15 Knavesmire	**What does lesbian look like?** The YLAF Debate. What is lesbian art in 2007? Do we still need it? Is there a lesbian anyway? Filmmaker [...] performance piece 'Out and into the Wardrobe.' After initial discussion by the panel, the audience will be invited to participate in the debate.
4.15	**Break:** Author & artist signings on 2nd floor
4.20-4.35 Voltigeur	**Fun & Funky Fresh Event:** "I'm Your Man!" Short performance piece with Julie McNamara. Comic monologue with raunchy song and a bit o' Leonard Cohen. Julie Mc, struts her stuff, ranting and raving in chameleon style to startling effect. She's raw, rare and rabid!
4.35-4.45 4.45-5.30 Voltigeur	**Announcements followed by:** On the pink sofa with... Crin Claxton gets comfortable with Jackie Kay, Stella Duffy & Sarah Waters.
4.35-4.45 4.45-5.30 Knavesmire	**Publishing:** Editors, publishers and self-publishers talk about getting into print. Kelly Smith, Tricia Walker & Ellen Dean with participating chair Jennifer Fulton.
5.30-6pm	**Book festival ends with final book signings on 2nd floor**

DJ Sadie Lee *(A-I)*

look like?' and asked 'What is lesbian art in 2007? Do we still need it? Is there a "we" in lesbian, anyway?' The audience joined in vigorously; the festival was, as Stella Duffy pointed out to me, a space where it was possible to have conversations around identity without the rancour that so often accompanies the issues today:

> I remember having a fantastic discussion one time, with Campbell, and Crin – about what butch is, about how I didn't identify myself as femme although they were framing me as such – about this borderline between 'is it ok to identify? Is it ok to self-identify? Is it ok to identify others? … and one of the things I thought was so important about that, was that it was a really deeply political conversation that could have gotten quite tense, or dark, or hard – and at the same time it was really loving. We had really *loving* political disagreements. And that makes me want to cry. Because we're so far from it now. There was this

DJ Claud Cunningham (A-I)

possibility of disagreeing around things that are really important in queer politics, without it putting us in such opposing camps that we weren't allowed to love each other. And I regret what I feel as the passing of that.

In changing times, YLAF's own definition of a lesbian remained broad and inclusive. The invitation to the Saturday dance night, Club Diva, read:

> This event is for women – and for those trans men (FTMs) and intersex people who are part of the women's community. As always, we welcome transsexual women whether pre- or post-op.

The club night filled two floors again. Claud Cunningham of Black Angel kicked off the night on Floor 1, followed by DJ Ad Astra; upstairs, the DJs were Emma Kirk and Sadie Lee.

On Sunday, in warm autumn sunshine, Claire Mooney, Helen Sandler, *a capella* group Deep C Divas, singer-songwriter duo

Readings from Charlotte Mendelson (top left) and Rhona Cameron; 'Fantastic Voyage' performance by Fiona Cooper

L to R: Jackie Kay, Stella Duffy and Sarah Waters, 'On the Pink Sofa'

Outdoor concert: Hiraani with balloons from the sponsor, Unison; drummer from Sista Slap

L to R: Jane Fletcher, VG Lee, Marianne K Martin and Ellen Dean on the 'What a Character' panel *(All photographs A-I)*

Secret's Out, and percussion band Sista Slap took to the outdoor stage. For Lynne Calvert, it was an unforgettable experience:

> Most of the time, I was an audience member, but in 2007 I performed in Secret's Out in York town centre! I shall never forget it; to look out over a sea of lesbians, most of whom had been at YLAF, was fantastic. Such a joy, an absolute honour! There were onlookers doing second takes, realising they were amongst so many LGBTQ people.

Crin and the team had pulled off a great festival against the odds. But with the financial crisis worsening, fundraising and finding increased sponsorship became even more pressing priorities for the board. Their efforts were successful; they could now plan for a return to the full four-day format in 2008.

Meanwhile, the cost of living continued to accelerate, and when tickets went on sale it rapidly became clear that even faithful YLAF supporters were having to think twice about whether they could afford to attend. Ticket sales in 2008 never made their target, and some fringe events had to be cancelled for lack of support.

Even so, no one who attended YLAF 2008 could have guessed, or expected, that this would be the last festival. Once again, the packed programme combined innovative events designed to

Enjoying the entertainment (A-l)

widen participation with the expected and much-loved staples – the book festival, workshops and concert. So the programme at the Racecourse began with a 'Love Lottery Night', hosted by Jean T, featuring matchmaking and relationship games, serenades from Aneesa Chaudhry and 'prizes and surprises' for the winners. The climax of the evening was a 'Blind Date' style game sponsored by Gingerbeer, in which the first prize was lunch with Val McDermid. Val still remembers her lunch partner as 'really nice and very good company', and the food, at York's only vegan restaurant, as 'diabolical'.

While I was collecting material for this book, some stories came up more than once, remembered by several different people. Aneesa lap-dancing Sandi onstage at the Barbican was one; Stella's performance of *Breaststrokes* was another; but the incident most often referred to involved Jackie Kay. Lynne Calvert told me:

> I remember quite a moment, with Jackie Kay and a small group of women in one of the lifts, listening to her reading poetry. She was doing poetry readings in the lift!

Lynne's partner, Viviana Archer-Todde, had a slightly different take:

> One of the happiest and funniest times we had at the event was actually getting stuck in a lift with none other than the future Scottish poet laureate, Jackie Kay! She had a biscuit tin which she occasionally rattled (don't ask me why) whilst she read some funny extracts from her books and some funny poems. We giggled so much and did not want to get rescued from the lift at all!

And Hilary Nowell told me:

> I can remember Jackie Kay reading a poem in a lift! Yes, going up and down. It was like a private reading… She's got class and style, and she could carry anything off, couldn't she?

As any oral historian will tell you, stories shift and settle over time, and people remember the same event in different ways. Were they stuck in the lift? Or was it a planned reading? Was Jackie reading poetry, or prose? Does it matter? Eventually, I heard the story from Jackie herself:

> I remember doing a reading one year, and we ran out of time. We had to read for exactly ten minutes, and I wasn't able to finish the story that I had started, and lots of people were really disappointed. So I said, half-jokingly, 'If anyone wants to hear the end of that story, I'll read it to them going up in the lift. That's the only space that's left that's not occupied!' I said, 'Meet me at the lift at 2 o clock.'
>
> And then I went to the lift, and there was a huge queue of people wanting to hear the end of this story! It was a joke, actually – I didn't expect anyone to be there – but there was a queue. So, I did that, taking six people up in the lift to hear the end of the story, and back down. Next six people: up, down. I think I must have done it about four times!

She added, with a grin:

> That was the first time I ever did something I would go on to think of as 'site-specific'.

Screenshot of the video evidence (LC)

'True Pride and Prejudice' (A-I)

When I consulted the relevant festival programme, I discovered that I'd had a hand in this story, too: with five writers of love stories to introduce in just three-quarters of an hour, I was the cruel panel moderator who had cut Jackie off in mid-flow.

The final twist in the tale came when Lenna Cumberbatch generously sent me all the photographs she had taken over the course of several festivals. Among the hundreds of images there are a handful of tiny, precious video clips. And there, on a Saturday afternoon in 2008, is Jackie, in close-up in a small space, giggling as she reads – to a chorus of laughs and gasps – a rather graphic sex scene set in a barn.

This year saw the return of the YLAF Playas with a new piece, 'The Puddle of Discontent' (a satire on Radclyffe Hall's *The Well of Loneliness*) as well as a repeat performance of the previous year's Jane Austen romp. Another innovation was the Queerlesque show at Club Diva. Acts ranged from leading cabaret performers to self-conscious first-timers from a YLAF workshop led by Killpussy, High Octane and Ingo from Club Wotever. All the acts were enthusiastically received by the club night audience, even though the majority had simply come clubbing rather than expecting to see any type of performance.

Naomi Young, founder and editor of the lesbian magazine *Velvet*, was at YLAF 2008 with her first novel *If It Falls*. In an article for the magazine shortly afterwards, she humorously described the atmosphere:

> One of the things I love about YLAF is that everyone, from attendees, to first time writers, to long-time little-known writers, to big names like Val McDermid and Jackie Kay, are all together very much on an equal footing. (Though it doesn't feel quite so equal when you're seated next to Val McDermid at the signing tables with your queue of, well… two!)
>
> I'd like to say I didn't feel out of my league on a panel entitled 'Are Lesbians the Only Fruit?' with Val McDermid,

Ingo of Club Wotever *(A-I)*

Justine Saracen and Stella Duffy, but I'd be lying if I did! But I didn't really need to say anything, when they said all I wanted to say, only more eloquently. I mean, you really can't sum up the thrust of the debate any better than Stella Duffy's answer: 'Are lesbians the only fruit? Absolutely not. But are they the fruit I prefer to eat/taste/bite/suck/lick/enjoy? Oh, yes.'

In spite of the punishing schedule and formidable financial challenges, Crin remembers her stint as festival director with great affection:

> Walking through the festival was the single most amazing feeling. I can't describe the energy of working all year round – in isolation most days, with just a monthly board meeting – and then seeing events come together, at the Racecourse, at the Opera House…

York's Grade II listed Grand Opera House was a seriously upmarket alternative to the Barbican Theatre, which remained closed. Filling the Edwardian auditorium with lesbians marked a high point of visibility for the festival (even though it was a nightmare for the disability access team). Programmed and introduced by Belinda O'Hooley, the concert featured the band Greymatter, comedian and singer-songwriter Clare Summerskill, American songwriter and multi-instrumentalist Erin McKeown, and standup comedian Jen Brister.

In all, sixty-five authors and artists from the UK, Europe and the USA appeared at YLAF 2008, and audience feedback ratings were very high: 97% described the festival overall as good or excellent. Sadly, though, in spite of the Board's best efforts, the event ended with a deficit, which had to be met from the organisation's small reserves, leaving no buffer against future financial challenges.

Planning for 2009 began straight afterwards, starting with the usual application to the Arts Council for the grant funding that had always kept YLAF afloat. In 2008, for example, the grant had been £39,000. Even though the organisers knew this support could not be taken for granted, it was a shock when, for the first time and in the worst possible circumstances, the Arts Council said no.

At the same time, the recession deepened further, becoming the most severe worldwide economic crisis since the Great Depression. It was a perfect storm: this financial climate, paired with the loss of Arts Council funding, spelled the end for YLAF. There was just enough money to pay off the company's debts, but no money for another festival. Exactly ten years after the opening of Libertas! bookshop, the YLAF story came to an end.

Maureen Elliott, who had served as treasurer since 2006, remembers:

> A small group of board members continued to try to raise funds for a few years, but it became obvious that this would not be successful, so in 2013 the decision to wind up the company was made.

It was a sad moment for everyone who had been involved with the festival. I remember talking to Jenny Roberts at the time, expecting her to be as upset as any of us – but, with characteristic Buddhist calm, she was the one who comforted me, saying, 'Everything has its time. And the festival was good while it lasted.' She was right. It has left us with good memories – and some souvenirs. Maureen Elliott told me:

> I still have – and use regularly – the mug produced for the 2008 festival by one of the board members, which listed all the artists who appeared that year. It's a piece of history.

It's a history that lives on, vividly, in the memories of thousands of festival-goers. ∎

The Grand Opera House entrance today *(Kate O'Dwyer)* and (below) the packed auditorium at the last festival concert *(A-I)*

Taking a final bow: 'The Puddle of Discontent' with (main picture L to R) Deni, Stella, Semsem, Helen, Crin and Robyn *(A-I)*

LEGACIES

AT THE VERY LEAST, the legacy of Libertas! and YLAF is a collection of happy memories. VG Lee summed it up:

> To be honest, a lot of the festivals have just merged into one memory, of a time of enjoyment. I don't remember the individual ones, but I remember the whole atmosphere, and what it meant to me: for once, going about in a large venue and not being in the minority. Going up on the train, you'd arrive at the London station and be looking out for lesbians; and you'd see lesbians and have a little smile through the crowds at each other; and your numbers slowly grew, and then you'd get off at York and there were masses of us! That's what the YLAF festivals really brought to us: we all had a weekend away, feeling like we were the majority. And that really was quite rare, then.

Val McDermid thinks such memories deserve to be preserved:

> It is important that our history is recorded, that it doesn't just slip away. And YLAF was important. I mean, how often in your life are you going to be sitting late at night with a bunch of women, two of whom were Dusty Springfield's lovers? It was full of those moments. And meeting people who are still my friends now.

Friendships made at York were a frequent theme in festival-goers' stories. Kate North echoed the experience of many women when she told me, 'I have friends and contacts still to this day because of YLAF.' That's certainly true for me: I met so many people over those years whom I'm grateful still to know. It was at YLAF that I met Hilary and Pauline Nowell, who not only became very dear friends, but contributed to (and became the 'cover girls' for) my collection of lesbian life stories, *Now You See Me*. Sometimes, it was not so much meeting new people, but meeting people in a new way: at YLAF 2003, I was unexpectedly reunited with a past pupil from my closeted teacher life, some thirty years before. As older adults, we have become good friends.

Elspeth Mallowan tells this happy story about meeting a work colleague unexpectedly at the festival:

> I was working for a rural charity, which involved meetings with the Countryside Agency and other local development agencies. There was someone I saw at a number of these meetings and my gaydar was alerted but, as we were highly professionally booted and suited, there never seemed to be the right moment to engage in personal chitchat. However, in 2006 at the Racecourse, I was rushing around as one of the organising team, sorting out volunteers at workshops and the consequent logistics, with a radio earpiece and clipboard in hand. I rounded a corner from one corridor to another, and bumped into her and her partner!
>
> There was what I can only describe as an exquisite moment of recognition and rejoicing, when the formality of our previous encounters was lifted and we embraced with sapphic joy! Subsequently, she and I have become good friends. We've both moved onto new roles in new organisations, but we have remained in regular touch.

Kate North reflected that the festival was a rare opportunity for cross-generational friendship:

> It was through YLAF that I got to know and meet many older lesbians, women who had hugely successful and interesting lives. I did not really know many older lesbians before that. It was inspirational to meet so many different

women who existed in sharp contrast with the way in which lesbians were represented in public discourse and the media at the time. For that reason, it was empowering, reassuring, and inspiring to me in my twenties.

Of course, the festival was a space for romance to blossom. Claire Mooney told me:

> In 2002, I'd just started to go out with Carol. We'd only just met, that September. (Love at first sight. Never believed it existed, then I met Carol. I'm going all woozy, thinking about it now.) And she was going to the event, and so we decided to go together. I played at the cabaret that year, and then stayed the weekend. So, we… had a nice weekend! And we've been together twenty-two years.

For Georgi Wootton-Badakshan, discovering Libertas! and YLAF was a 'turning point' in her life. She originally found out about the bookshop through other lesbian networks, and through being a fan of the American lesbian author and publisher, Radclyffe:

> First of all, I came across *The L Word*. Then, through that, I started reading *Uber L Word* stories online. And through that, I made contact with a Brit living in Belgium, who introduced me to Radclyffe's books and the online Libertas! bookshop. I read one of Rad's medical romances, then I joined her Yahoo! book group. I met loads of Rad fans in that group. I also met two women from Gothenburg, a married couple, who were avid LGBT readers.

When they discovered that Radclyffe would be appearing at YLAF, she and her Swedish friends, and another 'Rad group' fan from Stockholm, all decided to meet in real life in York.

> Meantime, I was now reading loads of LGBT novels and was enjoying *Tipping the Velvet* on UK TV. Karin Kallmaker

US authors Radclyffe and Karin Kallmaker
(Georgi Wootton-Badakhshan)

was also due to be going to York. I was so excited by all this, I hardly slept leading up to that weekend. It was liberating to encounter so many positive romances in the books, and the thought of meeting lots of like-minded lesbian readers was wonderful. At the Racecourse, there were so many wonderful authors and workshops.

On a personal note, I am lifelong friends now with Lisa and Mona in Gothenburg, who have shared so many authors with me and who remain two of my closest friends. I have visited them for traditional midsummer celebrations in Sweden twice and they have also visited Edinburgh a couple of times. We chat or text on a weekly basis and share photos or book recommendations.

My previous gay experience was several long-term relationships with women who preferred to stay in the closet, so it was very stifling and intense and ended badly. These days I have a number of gay friends, in Edinburgh and on Facebook, through YLAF and later the Nottingham

Bold Strokes book fests. I am in touch with a whole family of lesbian and LGBTQ friends worldwide. I am happier now than I have ever been.

But for me, the turning point was that first YLAF book festival. You just can't imagine how liberating that was. I was in my 40s before at last I was emotionally free.

The life-changing power of the festivals was especially felt by women who were, at the time, very new writers (or even just intending writers) themselves. In the early years, VG Lee was one:

> I think it gave me confidence. I must say that I probably realised for the first time that I could be funny. I had a big audience, not just like five or six in the backroom of a pub, and people thought me funny. And to be honest, I was 50 when I first did it and I was feeling older, and to have younger people as well thinking my work was humorous, and laughing and responding, it did me the world of good. It meant a lot.

Wollie Boehm (now better known as the award-winning lesbian romance writer Sam Skyborne) told me, 'YLAF was the start of my writing career!' She explained:

> I went to a Stella Duffy writing workshop as the 'plus one' to my partner at the time. On a Tudor pub crawl the following day, we drafted an idea for a novel. It became the first novel I wrote, though it was never published. I hope to publish it in 2025 as part of a series called 'Intel'.

I heard several accounts of the encouragement and empowerment fledgling authors received. For Nic Herriot, the volunteer who interviewed Alison Bechdel for *Diva* magazine, it was more a matter of clarification:

> Louise Carolin was really supportive to me. I'd been writing little things before that – I was writing for *Velvet*, I'd written a couple of short stories that got into *Diva* – and I was trying to build a writing career. Being a single parent is tough, but when Jude came into my life, I had the space, the mental capacity – and it allowed me to write. So, I'd done bits for local newspapers, and I was trying to get into *Diva* so I did lots of little bits and pieces for them...
>
> But Louise Carolin very gently said, 'Interviewing isn't your thing.' (My Alison Bechdel interview did get rewritten, at least twice.) And it's true, fiction is my forte. YLAF also made me realise I haven't got it in me to write a whole book. I'm a short story person. And that's what I do.

Singer-songwriter Lynne Calvert also feels that the festival impacted hugely on her creativity:

> Performing at the outdoor concert made me believe I could give things a go. Today I have developed my songwriting, then dared to think I am going to write a musical with a heavy LGBTQ+ focus. I've written all the music, and have a script in progress which I have been lucky enough to be successful in getting mentoring for, from Bradford Producing Hub. They are encouraging me to apply for further grants to keep developing the project. I honestly can say YLAF helped my development on that score. That's so precious to me and I cannot thank the festival enough. It would be interesting to know how many people developed projects through YLAF/Libertas's influence and inspiration.

It was more unexpected to hear that one of YLAF's established authors, Manda Scott, also had a life-changing experience because of the festival. For the last few years at York she was writing her *Boudica* series, in which shamanic dreaming is a central theme:

> But YLAF kicked me into teaching the Dreaming – which is

Manda Scott (A-I)

the single most important thing that has happened to me in my life – because I committed onstage to doing it.

I think I did two events – one on the Friday night and one on the Saturday – and I'm pretty sure someone came up to me on the Friday night and said something along the lines of, they didn't understand what it was. I said everything they needed to know was in the book, but they had said no, they didn't understand. And at the next event, the next day, I said, 'OK, I'm going to teach a group, so that you do all get it.' And almost all the people in that first group that I taught were lesbian women who had been to YLAF.

I honestly thought I would just do the one, and that would be it. And now I have an apprentice, and I think we are doing fifteen or sixteen groups a year… So, teaching the Dreaming arose out of YLAF. And that's been enormous. Totally life-changing.

Beyond the personal stories, there is perhaps a bigger legacy from the festival. Val McDermid certainly thinks so:

YLAF was tremendously important, not just because it brought us together, but also because it showed us what was possible. It was an extraordinary event. It wasn't just a bunch of lesbians getting together in a field; it was a proper book festival. It opened the door to a place in mainstream festivals, in mainstream cultural events. We were seen no longer as weird outliers, but as people who could contribute, majorly, to any event. And I think that's been one of the main takeaways from that period. It's not easy to persuade festival programmers to change their style, to change what they are doing, but YLAF made it possible for us to be able to persuade programmers to do things differently.

Even a cool Londoner like Chance Czyzselska recognised that something special was happening in York in those years:

I remember the vibe, and the excitement and the energy and the freedom, and having the whole of the Racecourse. It was lovely for me to get out of London, as well.

I can remember being there and just seeing this *sea* of lesbians, and *sea* of books. In a huge space, at the Racecourse. There was a bit of a joke about people wearing fleeces. Back then I was a bit of a fashion snob. And I did make jokes about the proliferation of lesbian fleeces, and how we should just make a fleece mountain in the centre of the Racecourse and burn it. But there was something about it. It wasn't cool; it wasn't hip or trendy, and maybe there was a bit of a London snob thing on my part about it… but who cares, right? It was a fantastic getting-together of lesbian and bi women on a huge scale, that wasn't that common at the time.

After that, there were *L Word* conventions and other TV things, and that kind of event took on a particular value. But then, it was a very rare occurrence, with so many women-loving women. It was quite a vibe – there was a sense of giggly freedom, almost – and it was different, because it

Chance Czyzselska DJing at Club Diva (A-I)

wasn't just centred round a nightclub. Clubbing, music and dancing were part of it, but people were there because they wanted to read lesbian literature, and meet people like them who were interested in lesbian authors. The literary aspect of it was really special and different.

I have fond memories of the festival – and I can recognise now, historically, the importance of it culturally for many lesbians.

For Claire Mooney, that importance was political:

YLAF was brilliant. People could be themselves. You could come out at an event like that. And it was safe. That was the biggest thing: it was safe. Even outside. So important – because in spite of all the Prides and everything, I still don't think it's that easy for people.

And it's amazing that YLAF led to other lesbian events. There was L Fest – I wouldn't be surprised if that was inspired by YLAF. Less so now: I think Prides have taken over. But Pride's sadly notorious for not always having that much lesbian input.

You're never sure how events like that touch people. And

how they meet up with others. It was a political event, whether we thought it was or not. Purely by us having the power, and holding an event like that – it was, in its own way, a massive political event.

Helen Sandler also picked up on the legacy:

> That time in my late thirties was one of the most productive times in my life, working for YLAF and *Diva*. I do look back at it with pride and some nostalgia. The experience I gained has fed into a lot of what I've done since. It allowed me to help bring an arts strand to L Fest, when Cindy Edwards set it up in Shrewsbury in 2011. It has also helped with running Tollington Press and with co-programming Aberration events here in Mid Wales, where Jane [Hoy] and I have lived for the past thirteen years. We moved west partly as a result of spending time in Shropshire at Jane T's. So the influences have continued for me.
>
> I'm trying to work less and do more fun stuff now, in my late fifties – and I'm about to put Tollington on ice – but I am still drawn to projects that put lesbian or LGBTQ+ people and stories centre stage. Other festivals have sprung up, and I enjoyed Out & Wild last year, but YLAF still has a special place in my heart. There was perhaps more demand for lesbian books and events than there is now. Regardless of whether there were always 3000 lesbians there, it was bigger than anything similar that I've been to since. *Diva* magazine claimed to have a readership of 90,000 in 2004 which would also be unheard of now.
>
> Ultimately we ran the festival for the community, for the women who came and took part, and the feedback was great. It meant a lot to people.

As a novelist, a board member and a hands-on volunteer over the years, Helen Shacklady saw the festival from every angle. She concludes:

I guess YLAF meant different things to different people. At the very least the festival was a place where women, whether 'out' lesbians or not, could be themselves and celebrate lesbian writers and performers together in public. It's easy to look back with rose-tinted specs and think that the early years of this century, not so long ago, were a more tolerant time, before debates about identity became so polarised. YLAF was inclusive, giving space to a wide range of women and also giving a voice, and an audience, to lesser-known writers and performers. If YLAF has a legacy, I would hope it is one of happy memories and of a time when women who probably did not all have the same views on various issues worked together to create something special. ■

Belinda O'Hooley and Heidi Tidow played an intimate Sunday luncthime gig to close the final festival (HS)

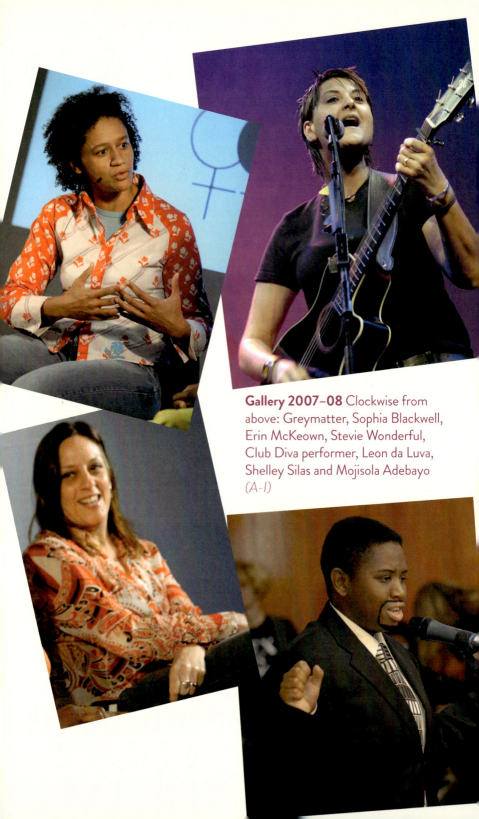

Gallery 2007–08 Clockwise from above: Greymatter, Sophia Blackwell, Erin McKeown, Stevie Wonderful, Club Diva performer, Leon da Luva, Shelley Silas and Mojisola Adebayo (A-I)

In the Company of Lesbians
Christine Webb

Christine after a reading *(LC)*

It was extraordinary to be for a few days in the company of so many lesbians. (This was the word we used generally at the time, often as a term of pride – it was of course part of the festival title.) There was a huge sense of camaraderie, a really festal atmosphere of jollity, rejoicing and – yes – relief. We were in the majority, we had nothing to prove or to defend: this must be what it feels like to be heterosexual. For some of us this was an almost uneasy feeling. We had grown so used to being on guard – and also, let's face it, we'd been proud of our minority status, our defiance of the norm. Let the straight world ignore, despise or attack us! We had our values, better values than theirs. This is not a healthy attitude to cultivate, however, even when you feel it's being forced upon you. But for this one weekend we could forget it.

And forget it we did, in the mix of serious entertainment and sheer fun. We'd be met by not just a buzz, but something more like a roar, from all the clashing voices in the canteen of York Racecourse, to which the festival soon moved. There would be a shriek of recognition as someone met a friend they hadn't known was coming: and some women made considerable journeys to get there – what's more it was November, not the most inviting month for travelling. Equally buzzy was the 'marketplace' selling themed merchandise, from key rings to engraved glasses (could you really get your names inscribed on them, or have I invented

FESTIVAL STORY

that?) And on the last afternoon of the festival there was a grand finale. I can still see the darting, almost dancing, figure of Sandi Toksvig, mic in hand, as she did a magnificent hour-long standup. She had acquired almost martyr status when Save the Children sacked her as their ambassador. The audience loved her and never stopped laughing.

As for the readings, talks and interviews with writers, they were packed. Val McDermid wasn't yet quite as nationally famous as she was soon to become, but her crime novels were already hugely popular, and we crowded into the room to hear her – wry, uncompromising, all wit and grit. A year or two later, Sarah Waters came, and the signing queue for her books snaked round several corners. That happened to be a year when I was reading, and we were signing at the same time. The contrast between our respective queues was like an anaconda beside an earthworm. Then there were panel discussions where two or three writers would take a particular angle, and the listeners joined in eagerly with questions and opinions. Writers never talked down to us or took up lofty positions – the atmosphere was democratic, even matey.

My partner Jackie was in a manual wheelchair the last time we went together, and we stayed in the disability suite of the Travelodge or Premier Inn, I forget which. In the middle of the night she woke up, stretched out for the light and set off the alarm instead. Bells rang, lights flashed and I leapt out of bed to ring reception and say it was a mistake – but I'd hardly got to the phone before the door opened and someone in uniform rushed in to save our lives.

The last two years I went on my own. One of them was to read from my first poetry collection, *After Babel*. I don't remember much about it except that, to my delight, my publisher, the late Harry Chambers [founder of Peterloo Poets], came to the reading. I didn't know he was going to be there – typical of Harry – and was entirely taken by surprise when at the end, after a couple of people had asked a question, he suddenly surfaced and asked me to read the last poem in the book. He was the only man in the audience. I sensed a slight bristling among some of the women at this intervention, and felt I must make clear that he *was* the great Peterloo Poets!

The last year, the date for YLAF was six months after Jackie had died. I was at the stage of accepting every invitation that was offered, and was given the chance of interviewing three authors, one of whom was Naomi Alderman, who had just published her first novel, *Disobedience*. I remember we had to time the event so that she could get back to London before dark, since it was Friday and Shabbat would be beginning. I also remember with lasting mortification that I had done some sound homework on my authors so that I could introduce them fittingly, but realised when unpacking that my carefully prepared notes were still on the kitchen table, a couple of hundred miles away. So I said airily to the authors, 'And now I'm going to ask you to introduce yourselves to the audience.'

I was a bit out of it, still, I think. Entire freedom, after a year of nursing and the expected death that followed it, had left me unanchored. What I remember most clearly of that weekend – apart from wearing a high-vis jacket and inexpertly directing in the car park – was pinning the 'Other Lives' obituary of Jackie that I'd written for the *Guardian* on a board in the canteen, and dedicating my part in the festival to her memory.

I seem to be finishing on a sombre note – but that would do the festival an injustice. We enjoyed it immensely, for all the reasons that I've said. Travelling there, through the toffee-coloured trees of autumn, there was always a tingling sense of anticipation, and driving back, a sense of warmth. I look back on it with pleasure and affection, and a sense of gratitude: how lucky I've been, to live at a time when such a thing could flourish. ∎

Leaf fall by the city wall *(Jane Traies)*

LIST OF AUTHORS AND PERFORMERS 2000–2008

BOOK FESTIVAL
Authors, speakers & workshop leaders

Naomi Alderman
Xenia Alexiou
RV Bailey
Kim Baldwin
Suzanne Batty
Alison Bechdel
Jay Bernard
Frances Bingham
Sophia Blackwell
Cathy Bolton
Amanda Boulter
Joanna Briscoe
Sarah Broughton
Rebecca Brown
Kathleen Kiirik Bryson
Campbell X
Clare Campbell
Rhona Cameron
Julie Cannon
Louise Carolin
Megan Carter
Maya Chowdhry
Crin Claxton
Rose Collis
Charlotte Cooper
Fiona Cooper
Helen Cross
Chance Czyzselska
Abha Dawesar
Ellen Dean
Stella Duffy
Cathie Dunsford
UA Fanthorpe
Marcia Finical
Jane Fletcher
Katherine V Forrest
Alma Fritchley
Jennifer Fulton
Ellen Galford
Frances Gapper
Jill Gardiner
Salena Godden
Michelle Green
Susan Hawthorne
Eleanor Hill
Jane Hoy
Linda Innes
Romi Jones
Karin Kallmaker
Ann Kaloski
Jackie Kay
Viv Kelly
Celia Kitzinger
Renate Klein
Helen Larder
VG Lee
Elizabeth Lewis
Reina Lewis
Jill Liddington
Mary Lowe
Lauren Maddison
Stacy Makishi
Aoife Mannix
Caeia March
Char March
Jane Marlow
Susannah Marshall
Marianne K Martin
Valerie Mason-John (Queenie)
Lisa Matthews
Lee Maxwell
Karen McCleod
Constance McCullagh (Hilary McCollum)
Val McDermid
Jenny Mckean-Tinker
Claire McNab
Karin Meissenburg
Charlotte Mendelson
Lilian Mohin
Raman Mundair
Inga Muscio
Kate North
Joan Opyr
Jacqueline Phillips
Cherry Potts
Radclyffe
Norrina Rashid
JM Redmann
Jenny Roberts
Lisa Saffron
Helen Sandler
Justine Saracen
Shamim Sarif
Manda Scott
Stacia Seaman
Helen Shacklady
Shelley Silas
Dorothea Smartt

Ali Smith
Kelly Smith
Virginia Smith
Cherry Smyth
Saradha Soobrayen
Diana Souhami
Jo Stanley
Al Start
Clare Sudbery
Therese Szymanski
Jay Taverner (Jacky Bratton and Jane Traies)
Stephanie Theobald
Lizzie Thynne
Sandi Toksvig
Louise Tondeur
Robyn Vinten / Ruby Vise
Tricia Walker
Helen Walsh
Sarah Waters
Christine Webb
Sue Wilkinson
Elizabeth Woodcraft
Erica Wooff
Naomi Young

PERFORMANCES
Performers, bands & DJs

Mojisola Adebayo
Patience Agbabi
Lorraine Ayensu
Black Angel (Claud Cunningham and Jag)
Jen Brister
Rhona Cameron
Chambers and Nettleton
Aneesa Chaudhry
Club Wotever (Ingo, Josephine and friends)
Deep C Divas
Dyke Marilyn
The Electric Landladies
Julie Felix
Deni Francis
Jess Gardam
Salena Godden
Greymatter
Halcyon
Deborah Hannah
Helen and the Lovenotes
High Octane
Horse
Izzy Isgate
The Jam Tarts
Jean the Clairvoyant
Killpussy
DJ Emma Kirk
Semsem Kuherhi
Amy Lamé
Sadie Lee
Rosie Lugosi
Leon da Luva
Mad Mandy
Maggie-Lou and Angie
Martha and Eve
Erin McKeown
Julie McNamara
Virginia McNaughton
Laura Meloy
Claire Mooney
The Moot
Never the Bride
Belinda O'Hooley and Heidi Tidow
Pauline Omoboye
Sue Perkins
DJ Ritu
Helen Sandler
Secret's Out (Lynne and Anita)
SheBoom
Karen Shook
Sista Slap
Al Start
Studio LaDanza
Clare Summerskill
Jean T
Sandi Toksvig
United Colours of Brooks and John
Vanilla
Rosie Wilby
Stevie Wonderful
YLAF Playas ∎

This list is drawn from the festival programmes. Those who appeared as part of a group are not individually listed; apologies to anyone else whose name is missing or has since changed.

ACKNOWLEDGEMENTS

3000 Lesbians Go to York is a testimony to the vision and energy of Jenny Roberts, without whom the festival would never have existed. So I want to put on record how grateful I am for her support throughout the writing of this book. It's been very reassuring to be able to check the details with her and Ann Croft as I went along, and to have access to their exhaustive Libertas! archive. (If I have made factual errors in spite of their help, the responsibility is, of course, all mine.)

Like my previous books, this one has been entirely dependent for its existence on the generosity of those who have contributed to it. Reconnecting with so many old friends and acquaintances and sharing our memories has been an enormous pleasure. So, thanks to everyone who wrote, texted, sent messages via social media, or agreed to be interviewed, either in person or online. Thanks, too, to everyone who sent me photos and videos, especially Lenna Cumberbatch and Crin Claxton, who emptied out their archives; and Vicky Morton, who helped to convert old video to an accessible format. Jim MacSweeney at Gay's The Word bookshop was generous as always with his expertise, and gave us valuable advice about the book's design.

While I was writing *3000 Lesbians*, some of the material I had gathered also became the basis for a documentary film; a selection of production stills closes this book. I'd like to thank Rachel Dax for taking that project on and, together with Kate O'Dwyer and Bonnie Rae Brickman, helping me tell the story in a different way.

As so many times before, I owe a special debt of gratitude to Helen Sandler: colleague and friend since before YLAF days, festival director for two years, and now my publisher at Tollington Press. Her input into *3000 Lesbians* has been beyond the usual call of duty for a publisher and editor, and invaluable because she was there from the beginning and knows, better than most people, just how it was.

IMAGE CREDITS

In the opening chapters, Jenny Roberts provided most of the images of Libertas! and early events; while Helen Sandler found pictures by herself and Kim Watson.

For the later festivals, most images are by two official photographers: Lenna Cumberbatch, whose portfolio is now archived at the Bishopsgate Institute; and Appature-Images. Kate O'Dwyer has provided film stills and shots of York.

Photographs are generally credited with the name of the contributor on first appearance, then with their initials, as follows:

    Appature-Images (A-I)
    Helen Sandler (HS)
    Jenny Roberts (JR)
    Kate O'Dwyer (KO'D)
    Kim Watson (KW)
    Lenna Cumberbatch (LC)

Other images are either credited on the page or provided by the people in the photographs. The author and publisher have endeavoured to acknowledge all photographs correctly, but would welcome the opportunity to correct or add credits when the book is reprinted.

We are grateful to Alison Bechdel for permission to reproduce 'Publish and Perish' from her 'Dykes to Watch Out For' series. ∎

'Now a Major Motion Picture': documentary version of *3000 Lesbians* in production (2024)

Clockwise from R: Val McDermid, Horse McDonald, VG Lee, Stella Duffy
(All film stills KO'D)

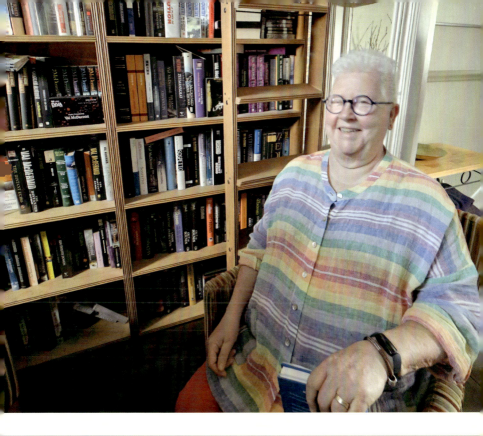

Lenna Cumberbatch and Jane Traies

Sarah Waters with (inset) co-producer Kate O'Dwyer

Diana Souhami reads from *Wild Girls*;
Crin Claxton and Helen Sandler reminisce
with Jane Traies, filmed by Vicky Morton

Aneesa Chaudhry with director Rachel Dax and (inset) crew

Jenny Roberts and Jane Traies

ABOUT THE AUTHOR

As an author and editor, Jane Traies has published *The Lives of Older Lesbians: Sexuality, Identity and the Life Course* (Palgrave Macmillan, 2016); *Now You See Me: Lesbian Life Stories* (Tollington, 2018); *Free to Be Me: Refugee Stories from the Lesbian Immigration Support Group* (Tollington, 2021); and other works in the field of ageing and sexuality.

As Jay Taverner, she is also joint author with Jacky Bratton of the Brynsquilver series of lesbian historical novels, which began with *Rebellion* (Onlywomen, 1997), *Hearts and Minds* (Diva, 2001) and *Something Wicked* (Onlywomen, 2002). The fourth in the series, *Liberty*, was published by Tollington in 2021, accompanied by new editions of the previous books.

Jane was deeply involved with the festivals in York for several years as an author and board member. She lives near Brighton.